Unions Resurgent?

Hobart Paperback 221

About IEA publications

The IEA publishes scores of books, papers, blogs and more – and much of this work is freely available from the IEA website: www.iea.org.uk

UNIONS RESURGENT?

The Past, Present and Uncertain Future of Trade Unions in Britain

J. R. SHACKLETON

Institute of
Economic Affairs

First published in Great Britain in 2024 by
The Institute of Economic Affairs
2 Lord North Street
Westminster
London SW1P 3LB
in association with London Publishing Partnership Ltd
www.londonpublishingpartnership.co.uk

The mission of the Institute of Economic Affairs is to improve understanding of the fundamental institutions of a free society by analysing and expounding the role of markets in solving economic and social problems.

A CIP catalogue record for this book is available from the British Library.

ISBN 978-0-255-36845-2

Many IEA publications are translated into languages other than English or are reprinted. Permission to translate or to reprint should be sought from the Executive Director at the address above.

Typeset in Kepler by T&T Productions Ltd
www.tandtproductions.com

Printed and bound by Hobbs the Printers Ltd

www.carbonbalancedprint.com
CBP2250

CONTENTS

ABOUT THE AUTHOR

J. R. Shackleton is Professor of Economics at the University of Buckingham and Research and Editorial Fellow at the Institute of Economic Affairs. He edits the journal *Economic Affairs*.

FOREWORD

During episodes of large-scale industrial action, the Institute of Economic Affairs receives media requests from TV or radio stations, which want to set up a debate between a supporter and an opponent of the strikes. Curiously, even when none of us have publicly commented on the subject, and media producers cannot possibly know what the position of anyone at the IEA is going to be, they just automatically assume that we must be in the anti-strike camp. Their thinking seems to be: the IEA is a classical liberal, free-market think tank, and being a free-marketeer means being 'anti-union'.

This is a fundamental misunderstanding, and if nothing else, I hope that Professor Shackleton's book on the history and the economics of trade unionism will help to clear this up.

A trade union is, in principle, a voluntary civil society association like any other, just like a tennis club, or the Campaign for Real Ale (CAMRA), or the Anglo-Hispanic bilingual meetup group. Thus, for a liberal free-marketeer to be 'anti-union' would make no more sense than for them to be 'anti–tennis club', 'anti-CAMRA', or 'against the Anglo-Hispanic bilingual meetup group'.

A classical liberal cannot be per se 'anti-union' (or, for that matter, 'pro-union'). They can only be against legislation that gives unions special privileges or coercive powers, for the same reason that they would be against legislation that gave tennis clubs or CAMRA special privileges or coercive powers.

In a free society, the right to set up or join independent trade unions – where 'independent' refers to independence from employers, but also from the state – is a fundamental and, from a liberal perspective, non-negotiable right. Countries which suppress those rights are not pleasant places to live: we can think of fascist regimes, military dictatorships, but also, ironically, self-described 'workers states', such as the former Soviet Union and its allies.

Conversely, where totalitarian systems are replaced by liberal democracies, this is usually accompanied by an emergence, or a return, of independent trade unionism. For example, in the Polish People's Republic, it was a trade union, Solidarność, which became a focal point of the civic resistance against the socialist regime in the 1980s. In (what would become) West Germany, a long tradition of independent trade unionism sprang back to life immediately after the defeat of the Nazi regime, and after the fall of the Berlin Wall, this was extended to East Germany as well. In Chile in the 1980s, the revival of trade unionism was one of the steps in the transition from military dictatorship to democracy.

We can, of course, imagine a free society without trade unions, just as we can imagine a free society without tennis clubs, CAMRA, or English–Spanish bilingual meetup groups, if there is insufficient demand for them. But the *right* to set up or join an independent trade union must always be guaranteed, even if it is not actively used.

From a more narrowly economic perspective, trade unions also have a perfectly legitimate role to play in a capitalist market economy. It is a completely normal arrangement in market economies that people with similar interests sometimes get together, and pursue their shared interests jointly, rather than individually. For example, homeowners may form residents' associations, and enter contractual relations with building companies, as a group, rather than individually. In the same way, a group of workers may decide that they want to negotiate aspects of their employment relationships collectively rather than individually. If all sides of the bargain agree with this arrangement, and enter it voluntarily, no supporter of free markets could have the slightest objections to that.

Where, then, does the misperception that free-marketeers are somehow hostile to trade unions come from?

Two reasons come to mind. Firstly, as mentioned, liberals object to special privileges for any group, irrespective of whether they sympathise with that group or not. At various points in British history, trade unions have enjoyed extensive privileges, and they arguably still enjoy some of those today. Where pro-market economists have said seemingly disparaging things about trade unions, they have done so in this specific historical context. Their statements should be read as such – not as a generalised hostility to trade unionism per se.

Secondly, while unions are not, in themselves, political organisations (any more than tennis clubs or CAMRA are), in practice, unions have often aligned themselves with left-wing political causes. That is, of course, their right – just as it would be the right of a tennis club, or of CAMRA, to align themselves with any political cause they may wish to align themselves with. But it means that they will sometimes clash with people who do not agree with that political cause.

But as Professor Shackleton also shows in this book, it is not always and everywhere the case that trade unions are part of the political Left. Historically, there have also been trade unions of various political persuasions, or none. There is also a tradition of trade unionism that is, if not explicitly classically liberal, then at least easily compatible with classical liberalism. Trade unionists in that tradition are fiercely protective of their independence, and they are hostile to state interference in labour markets, because they fear what might be called a 'crowding-out' effect. If employment relations are increasingly shaped by government legislation – who needs trade unions?

This strand of trade unionism seems to have gone extinct in Britain. But the insight that government action can crowd out trade unions remains relevant, and in a reverse conclusion, this also means that a weakening of the trade union movement may well be undesirable from a liberal perspective. Where trade unions recede, the space they vacate is not necessarily filled by voluntary free market arrangements. It is just as likely to be filled by even more

government regulation, and even more government interference in economic life.

But while this book is not – and, for the reasons described above, could not be – an 'anti-union' book or an
exercise in 'union-bashing', trade unionists and their
sympathisers will, of course, still find plenty in it to take
issue with. Professor Shackleton is immune to the trade
union romanticism that continues to dominate large
sections of the political Left, where perceptions remain
stuck in the days of Arthur Scargill and the Miners'
Strike. Union romantics still associate trade unionism
with coalminers and steel workers, when in 2020s Britain,
a trade union member is far more likely to be a relatively
well-paid white-collar public sector employee. Professor
Shackleton also shows that some of the economic benefits often ascribed to trade unionism are overstated or
non-existent, or may exist in a narrow sense, but are offset by less visible costs elsewhere. He shows that contrary
to fashionable opinion, the long-term decline in trade
unionism is not the result of a class war waged against
them, but simply a result of changes in the composition
of the economy. It is not unique to Britain, and it is not
easily amenable to legislative changes.

All in all, this book offers an account of the history and
economics of trade unionism which is often critical and
unsentimental, but never hostile, and not at all unsympa-
thetic. I hope that trade union members will read it in that
spirit.

The views expressed in this monograph are, as in all IEA
publications, those of the author alone and not those of

the Institute (which has no corporate view), its managing trustees, Academic Advisory Council members or senior staff. With some exceptions, such as with the publication of lectures, all IEA monographs are blind peer-reviewed by at least two academics or researchers who are experts in the field.

KRISTIAN NIEMIETZ
Editorial Director and Head of Political Economy,
Institute of Economic Affairs

SUMMARY

- Recent long-running and disruptive strike action has revived interest in a trade union movement which has been in long-term decline.
- Economists have always been in two minds about unions, seeing them as a possible countervailing power to over-powerful employers but also potentially using monopoly powers to distort labour markets.
- British trade unions have a long history; for many years their legal status was shaky and it was not until 1871 that members were free from the possibility of criminal prosecution and 1906 before union funds were safe from claims for damages for strike action.
- In the twentieth century two world wars led to the role of unions being enhanced and after the second war becoming an increasingly accepted part of the economic and political establishment.
- The post-war years, however, led to an arguably excessive growth in union power and influence that created problems for the UK economy and sometimes involved an unacceptable degree of coercion and disorder.
- Successive governments in the 1960s and 1970s attempted unsuccessfully to reform industrial

relations, with widespread strike action in the late 1970s culminating in the Winter of Discontent.

- Under Margaret Thatcher and John Major, militant trade unions were taken on and successive pieces of legislation clipped back their ability to disrupt the economy.

- Since then, there has been a long period of decline in union membership and the coverage of collective bargaining. This is not, however, unique to the UK, suggesting 'anti-union' legislation cannot be the only explanation.

- Today's union membership is very different from that in the past, with women now outnumbering men and with concentrations of union strength among well-qualified employees in the public sector or privatised industries which were once nationalised.

- Union membership still carries a wage premium and members also enjoy other employment advantages, but these advantages have been declining as across-the-board employment regulation has proliferated, supporting non-union as well as union workers.

- Unionised businesses display slow productivity growth and employment in non-unionised businesses grows faster.

- Strikes are now concentrated in the public sector, and they are aimed at inconveniencing the public in the belief that this is the best way to pressure governments to concede improvements in pay and conditions.

- There is unlikely to be a spontaneous revival in union membership, and attempts by government to encourage such a revival are not an effective vehicle for pursuing 'economic justice'.

- While unions have a legitimate role in the economy and civil society, serious disruptions to parts of the public sector where the citizen has no effective choice and where there is potential damage to health, safety and important government functions, may call for some restrictions.
- Governments in other comparable countries make use of compulsory arbitration and strike bans in some important public services. If we were to see a return to continuing costly disruption on the lines of the 1970s, these options might have to be explored even by a Labour government.

TABLES AND FIGURES

1 WHAT UNIONS ARE AND WHAT THEY DO

It is a basic problem of the place of trade unionism in society that those who view the union from within can genuinely and passionately perceive it so differently from those who view it from without.

Phelps Brown (1983: 48)

Henry Phelps Brown was on the money, and his words are as relevant today as they were four decades ago. People in unions taking strike action to restore or improve their living standards will always have a very different perspective from a general public who may be inconvenienced or damaged by strike action, but are not as intimately involved. Both, in turn, may differ from the view taken by politicians, economists, and others with a professional interest in how labour markets work.

The recovery of the economy after Covid lockdowns, coupled with rising inflation, was associated with a revival of trade union militancy and a spate of strikes from the spring of 2022 onwards. Those on strike at one time or another over the following 18 months included junior doctors, nurses, railway workers, barristers, schoolteachers, university lecturers, Border Force officials, offshore workers,

Royal Mail posties, civil servants, refuse workers, dock workers, airport staff, ambulance drivers, and many more. This led some commentators to suggest that we were facing a rerun of the late 1970s, when apparently never-ending strikes destroyed the economic policy of the Labour government, culminating in the 'winter of discontent'.

Unions had never gone away, but for many years they had been in decline, losing membership – particularly in the private sector and among younger workers – and political influence. Their bargaining power reduced, they rarely hit the headlines and the nightly news in the way that they had done 40 or 50 years ago, when union leaders were nationally known figures, regularly traipsing into Downing Street for crisis meetings, beer and sandwiches.[1] Will a rediscovery of militancy mean a revival of trade union power and influence, particularly with a new Labour government? We shall see.

Few of today's digital journalists were around in the unions' heyday, and often know precious little about the issues or the people involved. Nor do most of the general public. Yet the activists occupying the higher reaches of trade unions are often steeped in the history of the labour movement, and see today's disputes as the continuation of many generations of struggle.

---

1   This is not just a figure of speech. Beer and sandwiches began in Downing Street late on 12 February 1966, when Prime Minister Harold Wilson was negotiating with the National Union of Railwaymen over a threatened strike. Mary Wilson organised the sandwiches, borrowing bread from the Chancellor of the Exchequer next door as Number 10 Downing Street had run out (Wilson 1971: 275).

My intention in this small book is primarily to improve understanding of Britain's unions, what they do, their economic effects, strengths and weaknesses, and the position they continue to occupy in the political economy of the nation. And, with union actions now apparently back squarely in the political frame, I also offer some ideas about the choices which politicians face in dealing with revived union militancy.

What is a union?

Trade or labour unions exist in most countries. Although they have many elements in common with unions elsewhere, UK unions have a distinct history, philosophy and organisational structure. So we have to begin by clarifying what is meant by a trade union in the UK context.

A union in this country is an independent membership body, financed by its members, who are mainly in employment.[2] It is not a staff association or an exclusive professional body. Nor is it in itself a political organisation. To be registered by the government's Certification Officer, and hence obtain some important legal privileges, 'its principal purposes must include the collective regulation of relations with employers' (Certification Officer 2020). Its primary objective is to raise the living standards of members

---

2 Individuals may retain membership if they are retired, unemployed or otherwise out of the workforce. This is one of the reasons why membership figures reported to the Certification Officer will differ from those calculated from the Labour Force Survey, which estimates numbers of union members who are in employment.

through negotiating pay increases and improvements in working conditions. Many negotiations involve relatively harmonious discussions leading to a mutually satisfactory outcome. But they can also involve unions pressuring employers by withdrawing labour through strikes, working to rule, overtime bans and other forms of 'industrial action'.

A union may also have other functions, such as administering welfare and pension schemes, and offering legal and financial advice and assistance. They can also pursue political objectives, using a levy on members to support campaigns or political parties.[3] Most of the discussion here will, however, necessarily concentrate on 'collective bargaining', the term first used by Beatrice Webb[4] in the late nineteenth century to describe unions' central function.

Union immunity and the 'right to strike'

Registration is necessary to give a union legal protections and rights. Think about it: by organising strike action, unions are calling on members to break their contracts of employment. In common law jurisdictions – Australia

---

3   At the 2019 general election, for example, unions contributed just over £5 million of the £5.4 million registered donations to the Labour Party.

4   Beatrice and her husband Sidney were the first great historians of the labour movement. Sidney Webb (subsequently Lord Passfield) was a founder of the London School of Economics and later a member of two Labour governments in the 1920s and 1930s. The high-minded couple visited the early Soviet Union and became eager propagandists for what they regarded as 'a new civilisation' (Niemietz 2019: 63–69). It was certainly new, though not much of a civilisation. The Webbs were oblivious as late as the 1940s to the atrocities perpetrated by the Bolsheviks.

(McCrystal 2019: 131) is another example – this constitutes a tort, an action harming another party (the employer most obviously, but also customers, clients and the wider public). It therefore potentially gives rise to a civil case for damages – just as it would if a company broke its contract with a supplier or a client.

In some countries there is a legally guaranteed 'right to strike'. In France, paragraph 7 of the preamble to the 1946 constitution, later incorporated into the 1958 constitution, sets this out. In Spain, Article 28.2 of the 1978 constitution offers the same guarantee. In the US, Sections 7 and 13 of the 1935 National Labor Relations Act give the right to strike in pursuit of collective bargaining objectives.

It is often pointed out that there is no such right in this country. However, unions have, since the 1906 Trade Disputes Act, been granted immunity from legal liability for damages so long as the decision to strike meets various criteria.[5] These have been varied from time to time, most recently in the Strikes (Minimum Service Levels) Act 2023.

The action has to be in furtherance of a trade dispute, and it must be agreed by a formal paper-based postal ballot which is externally monitored. It must be directed at the employees' direct employer and not be a 'secondary' dispute in support of another group, must be notified to the employer in a timely manner, and cannot be undertaken to support an individual dismissed during unofficial industrial action. In addition, the 2016 Trade Union Act

---

5   The UK is not alone in qualifying the circumstances in which strike action is legitimate. France, Spain, the US and many other countries place conditions on legitimate strike action.

added some further conditions for a valid strike ballot, including a requirement that 50% of relevant members must vote in the ballot, while for workers in important services[6] the strike must have the support of at least 40% of those entitled to vote.

Unions do not simply negotiate pay and conditions for the relevant bargaining unit (including, incidentally, non-members). They also help individuals settle grievances, their officers accompany members to disciplinary hearings and support them at employment tribunals where they may be pursuing claims for unfair dismissal, discrimination or other breaches of employment law.

Where a union is formally recognised by employers (which may be a voluntary arrangement or, if the organisation employs at least 21 workers, determined by a decision of a body called the Central Arbitration Committee[7]), it will negotiate over pay and conditions, but also has a number of legal rights. These include the right to information and consultation over changes at work such as redundancies, and over health and safety. Workplace representatives of recognised unions are allowed paid time off for important activities such as negotiating changes to working

---

6 These services are health, education, fire, transport, nuclear decommissioning and border security.

7 This is a government tribunal, under the aegis of the Department for Business and Trade. It originally had a wide range of responsibilities (Gouldstone and Morris 2006) but now focuses on union recognition (and derecognition). Since 1998 a union can apply to the Committee for recognition, claiming that at least 50% of those in the relevant 'bargaining unit' want union recognition. The CAC can award recognition on the basis of evidence presented by the union, or by holding a ballot.

conditions and accompanying members at disciplinary or grievance meetings.[8]

These rights and immunities were not created all at once. As the next chapters show, they are the product of more than two centuries of activism by unionists, resistance by employers and frequently changing government policies. Many aspects of current industrial relations law are still contentious, and will likely remain so. The recent rash of strikes provoked some Conservative politicians to demand tighter restrictions on the conditions under which strike action is permitted. On the other hand, the Labour Party has indicated that, on returning to power, it will repeal some Conservative trade union legislation, making it easier to take industrial action and encouraging a revival of union membership.

As F. A. Hayek pointed out many years ago, the most fundamental aspect of trade union law is this ability to strike with statutory immunity from civil action. The immunity may have been redefined on multiple occasions, but it remains a key element of union power.[9] While the ability to strike remains widely accepted, there are both classical liberal and pragmatic grounds for keeping it constantly under review. Even the principle is not beyond challenge. For some classical liberals (for example, Epstein

---

8   https://www.gov.uk/rights-of-trade-union-reps

9   Unions can also use political clout arising from organised workers to press politicians, at local and national level, to make decisions favourable to their interests. Organised representation by police and prison officers, despite not allowed to strike, can still be influential – especially when the law gives them the right to be consulted over matters such as health and safety and redundancies.

1984, 2012, 2013), the protected legal status of unions is an unjustifiable interference with freedom of contract, freedom of association and property rights.

Hayek (1960: ch. 18) observed that protection against liability for damages gives unions a degree of power to coerce employers – and sometimes also unwilling employees. In this view, unions act as a sort of monopoly supplier of labour, and like all monopolies this can have a pernicious effect on the economy. Immunity may enable powerful unions to impose a pattern of wages and other conditions which can be economically inefficient, damage productivity, create unemployment, facilitate inflation and ultimately pose a significant threat to individual liberty. In a famous letter to *The Times* in 1977, Hayek wrote that 'there is no salvation for Britain until the special privileges granted to the trade unions by the Trade Disputes Act of 1906 are revoked'.

Why do people join unions?

But just how does a union acquire sufficient power to induce employers to alter the pay and conditions of employment they would otherwise choose to offer? And, more fundamentally, how does a union even get started? The historical development of British unions is described in the next chapter. However, it is also worth considering union formation in more abstract terms. Economists have devoted some attention to this: it is not self-evident.

In a trivial sense, people who voluntarily join unions do so because they expect the benefits to exceed the costs. Some people join unions because they are committed to an all-consuming political struggle; in economists' terms they gain 'utility' directly from this involvement. British unions have rarely been short of left-wing activists whose objectives go beyond improving their own pay and conditions to seek fundamental changes in the economic system. But the bulk of members have always been much more instrumental in signing up to a union. They must be expecting that the costs they incur – primarily financial in modern conditions[10] – will be more than covered by the returns to collective action.

But thinking about these returns raises questions. First, in order for unions to be able to secure higher pay from private sector[11] employers, these employers must themselves possess some degree of market power which enables them to be making 'rents' or supernormal profits – that is, profits greater than those which just allow them to stay in business. Otherwise, any higher pay unions obtained would be short-lived. A successful union is, in effect, redistributing rents from shareholders to employees. We would not expect unions to be able to secure significantly higher pay from small firms in highly competitive markets, such as local privately owned restaurants, shops, garages or hairdressers, where rents are close to zero.

10 These are principally the costs of membership fees and the expected costs of lost pay during strike action. Until comparatively recently, however, unionists may also have faced the risk of penalties such as losing their jobs for being members of a union (now forbidden by law) or, in the nineteenth century in particular, the risk of prosecution, fines and possible imprisonment.

11 The public sector is a different matter, as government-funded employment is not subject to market discipline in this way. This is discussed in a later chapter.

Second is another fundamental difficulty for unionism: the fact that the benefits from successful union action are collective rather than purely private gains.

In his influential book *The Logic of Collective Action,* the American economist Mancur Olson (1965) argued that desirable collective action, including union action, resembles the 'public good' which was defined in the 1950s by Paul Samuelson (1954) and Richard Musgrave (1959). Collective goods, like public goods, are non-rival and non-excludable. A union-negotiated wage increase benefits all employees in a group – thus non-rival – and it is non-excludable because allowing some workers to be paid less would undermine the union's bargaining position. Thus, union pay settlements are typically paid to all workers in a group, whether union members or not. This gives rise to the classic 'free rider' problem, where an employee can take the benefits of collective action without incurring the costs. Too many free riders, and your union will not get off the ground.

For Olson and later analysts, any successful collective action – such as the formation of a union – is unlikely to happen in the absence of two conditions (Willman et al. 2020: 250). The first condition is the provision of 'selective incentives': private benefits to members which are not available to non-members. The early trade unions, as the next chapter indicates, were often built on 'friendly societies', simple informal mutual associations providing support to members in illness or old age.[12] In modern conditions, the state has largely taken over such responsibilities.

---

12 Hayek, incidentally, approved of this role for unions.

However, in addition to the important provision of legal[13] and practical advice for a member's grievance or dismissal problems, unions continue to offer members a range of less obvious private benefits. The Unite website, for instance, shows that this union offers a will-writing service, mortgage advice, a dental plan, accidental death cover, holiday offers, savings plans, RAC breakdown cover, travel and car insurance, and various consumer discounts.

Unions may be able to provide such services cheaply because they can forge deals with providers, based on scale economies which are not open to individuals.[14] So in this story, union collective benefits (improved pay and working conditions) are a 'joint product' with private benefits.

The second, more sinister possibility is the ability to exercise coercion. Olson (1965: 75) drew attention to 'compulsory membership and coercive picket lines'. Such compulsory membership was a feature of the 'closed shop' (where you had to be in a relevant union to hold your job), common in Britain in the 1960s and 1970s though now illegal. This practice only became widespread after unions were already powerful, and then only in a section of the labour market. But it had its roots long before. There are records in the National Archives (2019) of an 1820 legal case where Samuel Starling, a maker of ladies' shoes, lost

---

13 Union officials often know more about the law than employers, particularly in smaller businesses.

14 As Booth (1985) points out, in theory, a business could package all these benefits and sell them, without the collective benefit (which is costly to provide), at a lower price than union dues. Perhaps, though, union members have a demographic which is more attractive to providers of these services than would be achieved by offering them in an open market.

his job after falling behind with his subscriptions to a society of Journeyman Shoemakers. His fellow workers told the employer they would not work with him, so the employer dismissed him.

More will be said on this sort of overt coercion later in the book. More subtle, perhaps, is the social pressure which groups can exercise, particularly if you live in isolated areas where a particular employer dominates – for example in the mining villages of the nineteenth and twentieth centuries. Booth (1985) developed a formal model of such pressures, where individuals gained utility from their reputation – of being part of the collective rather than a 'scab', who dares to undermine a strike by continuing to work.

Perhaps coercion is rather too strong a term for what is a common human impulse. In any community there are inevitably demonstration effects in everything from consumer choice to religious observance to membership of a political party. This is not usually seen as coercion or oppression, and nor is union membership in most circumstances. In the past, such membership was often the norm, which new workers accepted without thinking, just as they might have gone to church on Sunday. With social change and greater population diversity, however, this is not necessarily the case anymore. It may take specific action to stimulate willingness to join.

An interesting take on this is provided by Hodder et al. (2017). These authors review possible factors influencing unionisation; these include the resources unions devote to recruitment, the sense of injustice workers may feel at current pay and conditions, the belief that unions can be effective in securing improvements, and pro-union social norms. They argue that these factors will be enhanced during periods when unions are organising strike action.

Using data from a large civil service union with a record of frequent strike action over a seven-year period, they find (after controlling for other possible determinants of membership) that in months where there is strike action, membership rises. Recruitment increases, while the number of 'leavers' falls. While it's a popular assumption that greater unionisation leads to more strikes, the causation may also run in the opposite direction. Certainly, there are historical instances where we can point to such an effect. It is yet to be seen whether recent increases in strike action lead to a significant upturn in union membership.

Union objectives

There is a long tradition of seeing workers as fundamentally disadvantaged[15] in the labour market. In the context of disputes between workers and employers, Adam Smith (1776: ch. 8) wrote:

> It is not, however, difficult to foresee which of the two parties must, upon all ordinary occasions, have the advantage in the dispute, and force the other into a compliance with their terms. The masters, being fewer in number, can combine much more easily; and the law, besides, authorizes, or at least does not prohibit their

---

15 For a contrary view, see Epstein (1984).

combinations, while it prohibits those of the workmen. We have no acts of parliament against combining to lower the price of work; but many against combining to raise it. In all such disputes the masters can hold out much longer ... In the long run the workman may be as necessary to his master as his master is to him; but the necessity is not so immediate.

Not everybody would agree with Smith's analysis. Hutt (1954: 44–55), for example, points out that the evidence for employer combinations, certainly in Smith's time and for most of the nineteenth century, is thin on the ground.

Nowadays the argument is not so much based on employer collusion, but rather in terms of particular employers possessing a degree of monopsony power. A pure monopsony, the term introduced by Joan Robinson (1933), is a 'single buyer'. In the labour market it means an extreme position where there is only one employer in the relevant part of the market, and workers have to take the wage they are offered because they have no alternative employment possibility. This wage is lower than that which would obtain if there were competition for labour. Figure 1 is the standard textbook diagram illustrating such a situation.

If there were many employers competing for workers, the wage (W_c) and employment (Q_c) would be determined by the intersection of demand and supply curves. If we have a monopsony, the demand curve, determined by the marginal revenue product of labour[16] (MRP) represents the

---

16 The addition to total revenue generated by employing one extra unit of labour.

single employer's demand. The supply curve now shows the employer's average cost of employing labour (AC_L). As this is rising with increases in employment, the cost of each extra unit of employment must be greater than the average cost, so the curve showing the marginal cost of labour (MC_L) lies above the supply curve.

Figure 1 Monopsony in a labour market

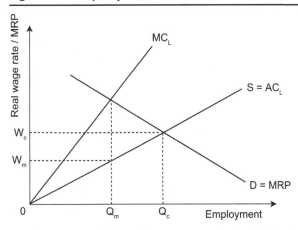

The monopsony employer maximises profits by employing up to the level where the MC_L is just equal to its MRP. The MC_L and MRP curves cross at employment Q_m. At this employment level, the employer will pay a wage of W_m, which we read off from the supply curve. This wage is less than labour's MRP, and is less than the competitive wage (W_c) would have been. The employer makes supernormal profits as a consequence, something most conventional economists would see as a form of market failure.

The implication is that in these circumstances, the introduction of a powerful union could act as a counter-vailing power against the employer, and raise both wages and employment. This could bring this part of the labour market closer to what a competitive outcome would have been. As Dodini et al. (2021: 2) put it:

> [U]nions may be able to correct an existing market failure by counter-balancing the monopsony power of employers, raising wages and pushing ... closer to the competitive equilibrium, ultimately generating a more efficient allocation of resources conducive to higher economic growth.

It is debatable how significant monopsony in labour markets can be in modern conditions. Many economists believed until recently that globalisation and increased competition had made monopsony, in the private sector at least,[17] a thing of the past. Some recent research (Sorensen 2017; Abel et al. 2018) has suggested, however, that it may be more common than was thought.

If one of the attractions of the monopsony model for academic supporters of trade unionism, such as Alan Manning (2003), is that it suggests union power can have a positive effect on the economy by pushing wages and employment closer to competitive levels, another is that union workers' wage gains come at the expense of supernormal

---

17 However, something approaching monopsony may exist in parts of the public sector. The National Health Service, for example, is the employer of a very large proportion of some types of medical personnel.

profits. This may seem to obviate concern that there is any necessary trade-off between higher pay and employment.

But in the absence of monopsony, union negotiators face the reality that significantly higher wages will probably mean fewer jobs. There is no simple understanding of how they handle such a situation. In a democratic union, some workers will push for higher wages and ignore the risk that they might lose their jobs – while others are likely to be more cautious. Many economists have assumed that the preferences of the 'median voter' – probably a relatively senior employee – will dominate, and have speculated on their attitude to risk. Others disagree that ordinary union members have much influence. They point out that, on the one hand, union officials may be able to impose their own, possibly rather conservative,[18] preferences, while at the other extreme, the union's strategy may be seized by militants pursuing a radical political agenda.

Whatever the case, a mainstream approach assumes that the union's preferences, however determined, can be represented by indifference curves, as in Figure 2. All points along a curve, representing different combinations of wage rate and unemployment, give the same level of utility. The union aims to be on the highest possible indifference curve, representing the highest level of utility. In this diagram, the labour demand curve serves as a constraint facing union negotiators. The competitive market wage, in the absence of union activity, is W_P. The union prefers

---

18 Officials, with a better understanding of market conditions and a wish to maintain membership numbers, may not want to risk jobs by excessive wage demands.

W_M, which is on a higher indifference curve. This involves a lower level of employment (E_M) than would otherwise be the case (E_P).

Figure 2 The union trade-off

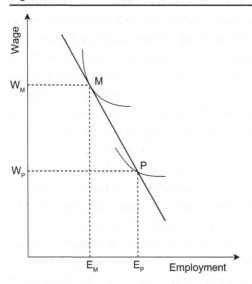

If the union has an effective monopoly on the supply of a particular type of labour and can achieve its preferred outcome, this model suggests that there is in consequence a lower level of employment and output, and that some workers are shifted into lower-productivity (and lower-paid) non-union jobs. This displacement of labour and distortion of the wage structure is a key element in economists' concern that union power reduces economic efficiency. The extent of this effect will depend on the wage elasticity of demand for labour, a topic first explored by Alfred Marshall (1920: 319–20) and further explored by Sir John Hicks (1963: 241–46). While critics of unions have asserted for many years that this distortion seriously damages the economy, others, such as Milton Friedman (1962: 123–24) have been less certain.

Figure 3   Being off the demand curve can create an 'efficient contract'

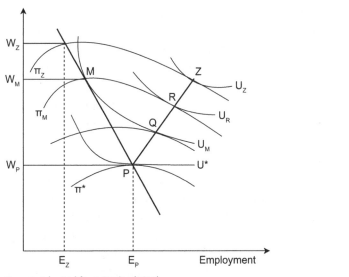

Source: Adapted from Borjas (2013).

The thinking behind Figure 2 assumes that unions are able to impose a wage as a result of their quasi-monopoly power, and the employer simply reacts to this by setting the (reduced) level of employment. This is often referred to as a 'right to manage' model: the union is only interested in pay, and leaves management free to set hours and/or numbers of employees. However, a more sophisticated analysis, as shown in Figure 3, qualifies this argument. It suggests that negotiation over employment as well as pay between a monopoly union and the employer could lead to an 'off-the-demand-curve' solution which would be preferred by at least one of the parties.

Here curves U^* to U_z are indifference curves representing the preferences of union decision-makers between combinations of wage and employment. The curves π^* to π_z are isoprofit curves showing combinations of wage rate and employment which will give the same level of profit. The firm wants to be on the lowest possible isoprofit curve as this represents the highest level of profit.

At the competitive wage w_p the firm makes maximum profit. But the union is on the low indifference curve U^*. If it is powerful, it can push the wage up to W_M where indifference curve U_M is tangential to the demand curve, as in Figure 2. It is better off than at the initial position. However, it could do still better if it could get the firm to move off the demand curve to a position such as R. This is on a higher indifference curve, U_R, and the union would be better off – while the firm, still on isoprofit curve π_M, is no worse off. Alternatively, the firm could try to persuade the union to move to position Q. The union is no worse off than at M, but the firm is on a lower isoprofit curve (i.e. makes a higher profit).

All the possible 'efficient bargains' are traced out by the line PZ, which is termed the contract curve. The limits are at Z (at a level of profit π_z, below which the firm would go out of business) and P (at which the union would be no better off than at the market wage rate). Where exactly on the contract curve the bargaining parties end up is unclear. There is a considerable literature on this question, but as Borjas (2013: 437) puts it, 'there is no widely accepted model of the collective bargaining process showing how a particular point on the contract curve is chosen'.

Although the outcomes cannot be predicted, if the contract curve looks like that in Figure 3, any point between P and Z will mean that employment is higher than the competitive level or, to put it differently, there will be overstaffing, another aspect of the inefficient allocation of labour.[19] The bargain reached may be an 'efficient contract' in that a move to a different position will make either the union, or the firm, or both, worse off. But it is not efficient from a wider perspective.

Which of these approaches – the 'right to manage' or the 'efficient contract' models – is most plausible? Recent research in the UK has rarely examined this explicitly. However, a paper (Fanfani 2023) covering Italian collective bargaining from 2006 to 2016, is suggestive. The author finds that (ibid.: 17)

> collective bargaining has a positive influence on wages and a considerable negative effect on employment ... negative employment effects were prevalent among young

---

19 Unless the shape of the isoprofit and indifference curves is such that the contract curve is vertical. In this case employment will be at the socially optimal level and all union gains will be at the expense of supernormal profits.

workers, fixed-term contracts, those currently unemployed, and relatively less efficient firms ... Italian collective bargaining seems well characterized by models where firms set employment according to their labor demand, rather than on an efficient contract ... the standard Hicks–Marshall theory provides several predictions consistent with our results.

More will be said about the empirical evidence on the effects of unions in a later chapter. But having sketched some of economists' ideas about unions, we now turn to the historical development of union power in Britain.

2 TRADE UNIONS IN BRITAIN: FROM EARLY YEARS TO THE MID TWENTIETH CENTURY

In the previous chapter the formation and objectives of trade unions were discussed in the abstract. But unions in twenty-first-century Britain, and their often antagonistic relationship with employers and the government, have not just arrived here in Doctor Who's Tardis. They cannot be understood without some grasp of their historical development. Struggles and confrontations of the past, and the stories told about them, still inform today's attitudes, and continue to cast long shadows. In this chapter I aim to outline the key features of the early development of British trade unionism and its legal implications.

Trade unions have a history in this country stretching back, at least in rudimentary form, to the seventeenth century. Notice that word 'trade', which indicates early unions' origins among workers in particular crafts or trades.[1] The label 'union' was not widely used at first; groupings of workers defending their interests and seeking increases

---

1   For example, organised workers were active in the printing and papermaking trades in the second half of the eighteenth century. In 1786, 24 London bookbinders were prosecuted for conspiracy after striking for a reduction in the 14-hour day (Burke and Field 2023).

in pay and improvements in conditions were most often referred to as 'combinations', particularly by their critics. Their legal status had been perilous from the start. Some groups of workers sought to disguise their intentions by the formation of those innocuous-sounding 'friendly societies' mentioned earlier – legally permitted mutual associations which offered their members informal contribution-based insurance against illness and unemployment, or provided burial expenses.[2]

The Combination Acts

Combinations, whether of workers or employers, were long anathematised as a restraint on trade, distorting markets. But it was workers who were most at risk from the law. In the course of the eighteenth century several Acts of Parliament sought to ban combinations of workmen in particular trades and occupations (Orth 1987). Where there was no specific legislation, common law offences such as conspiracy could be used to penalise workers who might be fined, jailed or even transported to the colonies.

Following the French Revolution in the late eighteenth century, and during the subsequent Napoleonic Wars, fears of internal subversion and possible imitation of France's

---

2 'Workers combining for wage bargaining purposes, which were of doubtful legality, could use the organisation of a friendly society as a legal mask for their activities' (Pelling 1992: 11). It was a flimsy protection: the Tolpuddle Martyrs, Dorset farm workers convicted of swearing an illegal oath and transported to Australia in the 1830s, were members of the Friendly Society of Agricultural Labourers.

revolutionary terror led to the imposition of general laws against combinations.

The 1799 'Act to prevent Unlawful Combinations of Workmen' consolidated legislation in particular trades into an across-the-board ban on combinations. It was quickly superseded by the 1800 Act, which allowed for arbitrators to settle disputes, failing which employers and workers might appeal to a magistrate, but maintained prison sentences for breaches of the law.[3]

Despite the new legislation, groups of workers continued to engage in collective action, sometimes linked to underground political movements. Prosecutions were occasionally brought under the new Acts, but more often conspiracy charges or other pre-existing laws were invoked.

The Combination Acts became the object of considerable opposition from workers and radicals, but also from campaigning Parliamentarians such as Joseph Hume and Sir Francis Burdett, and economists such as J. R. McCulloch (Grampp 1979; Fetter 1980: 65; Hupfel 2022). In 1824 the laws were repealed, but this was rapidly followed by a rash of strikes. Several petitions then called on the politicians to restore the status quo ante. Parliament had second thoughts, and in 1825 a new Combinations of Workmen Act was passed. Rather less harsh than the earlier laws, this new legislation at least now permitted nascent unions to bargain over wages and conditions although it still allowed strikers to be prosecuted for criminal conspiracy, including picketing.

---

3   The law also forbade combinations of employers, but I have not been able to trace any cases where this aspect of the legislation was invoked.

The Victorian age

As the scale of industry grew, with the development of large factories, concentrations of workers and concomitant profits, the possibilities for effective unions increased. Already by the 1820s and 1830s, attempts were being made to form national general unions. One such was the Operative Builders Union (a federation of seven building unions with strengths in London, Birmingham, Manchester, Liverpool and Newcastle). A better-known example was Robert Owen's Grand National Consolidated Union (founded in 1834), which attracted early socialists and took a strong political line. But these unions did not last. Attempts to broaden unionism at this time were to some extent overshadowed by Chartism, the great working-class movement for political reform. The demands of the People's Charter were for manhood suffrage, equal electoral districts,[4] voting by ballot, annual parliaments, abolition of property qualifications to become a member of Parliament, and payment for MPs.

Despite their uncertain legal position and many organisational difficulties, unions were to make great progress during the long reign of Queen Victoria. By mid century, craft-based organisations, christened the 'new model' unions by Sidney and Beatrice Webb (1920: ch. 4), had achieved a considerable degree of respectability. These outfits represented a single craft (the Amalgamated Society of Engineers, the Amalgamated Society of Carpenters) and

---

4   At that time, some emerging industrial districts where unionism was developing – such as Birmingham – had no Parliamentary representation.

were for skilled workers who emerged from a time-served apprenticeship, had a scarcity value, and maintained pay differentials with demarcation from unskilled workers.

Craft workers such as these were already reasonably well-paid by the standards of the time. This meant that their unions could charge meaningful membership subscriptions and support full-time officials – and even premises in London, where they sought to influence Parliament. They had formal branch structures and took a long-term view, aiming to avoid unnecessary strikes and hostility between workers and employers. Their officials began to meet on a regular basis and their meetings eventually gave rise to the London Trades Council[5] and later the Trades Union Congress (TUC), founded in 1868.

A number of legislative interventions improved the position of unions during this period, including the 1855 Friendly Society Act (giving legal protection to benefit funds) and the 1859 Molestation of Workmen Act (which legitimised peaceful picketing[6]).

Their status was further enhanced as a consequence of the Royal Commission on Trade Unions, set up in 1867 by Lord Derby's Conservatives in response to the 'Sheffield

---

5 Trades councils are local bodies bringing together unionists from different industries to campaign over issues affecting workers. There are still around 150 trades councils in England and Wales (TUC 2019).

6 Picketing involves striking workers (and sympathisers) gathering outside a place of work to discourage non-strikers from entering, and to advertise their grievance more widely. In the nineteenth century its legal status was doubtful, while mass picketing (often involving violence or the threat of violence) was banned after the 1926 general strike, legalised after World War II, and then banned again after the events of the 1970s and 1980s.

Outrages'. Downing (2013: 162) describes these as 'a series of high-profile violent attacks by workmen in the Sheffield light metal trades on fellow workers and employers.' This reminds us that the respectability of the new model unions coexisted with darker, more desperate, worker activism. The secretary of the Sawgrinders Union, for example, is said to have evaded prosecution despite admitting the solicitation of an employer's murder. Today, a hipster bar in Sheffield keeps the union's name alive.

Although the Royal Commission's majority verdict was against decriminalising union activity, the minority report's proposals were in favour. And it was these minority proposals which were to be taken up by the Liberals when they returned to power and produced the Trade Union Act of 1871. This clarified unions' legal position, supposedly freeing members from the possibility of criminal prosecution and protecting their funds.

However, ambiguity in the Act, plus conflicting legislation on picketing passed in the same year, led to further legal changes. This time it was the Conservatives, back in office under the more worker-friendly Benjamin Disraeli, whose 1875 Employers and Workmen Act began to replace the old 'Master and Servant'[7] principle with a formal equality of status in a contractual relationship.

---

7   If the Combination Acts were directed against collective action, legislation such as the Master and Servant Act of 1823 had affected individuals, specifying prison sentences of up to three months for absconding from work. It now seems barely credible, but as late as the 1860s there were still 10,000 prosecutions a year under this Act. There was some overlap with anti-union legislation: union officials could be caught with Master and Servant Laws as they attempted to organise breaches of contract.

If the mid-Victorian years saw the rise of a craft-based unionism, the later nineteenth century was to see the growth of different types of organisations. Operatives' unions for semi-skilled workers grew up in such occupations as mining and textiles in the 1880s, and a little later came the emergence of the 'new unions'.

According to the Webbs, this 'new unionism', bringing in mass membership of semi-skilled and unskilled workers, with low union dues and without friendly society benefits, began with the London dock strike of 1889 – though some, for example Duffy (1961), claim that the movement began earlier. In any case, the 30,000 members of the Dock, Wharf, Riverside and General Labourers' Union won significant advances in wages and working conditions.

This kicked off a new era in trade union power and influence. Union membership of both skilled and unskilled workers grew rapidly, from around 750,000 (6.2% of employees) in 1888 to 1,576,000 (13%) in 1892. This trend was a factor in the establishment of a new Royal Commission on Labour, which ran from 1891 to 1894. The great economist Alfred Marshall (Groenewegen 1994) was a member of this Commission, which, while not making any major recommendations, nevertheless foreshadowed what later became industrial relations orthodoxies. Thus it favoured collective bargaining ('joint regulation') of pay and conditions, and rejected interference by the state. For example, it argued against compulsory arbitration or making collective agreements legally enforceable.

But if the Royal Commission argued for non-intervention (or what later came to be called 'voluntarism'), other developments around the same time nevertheless involved some important extensions of government regulation. In 1891, for example, the House of Commons passed the first Fair Wages Resolution.[8] This required employers working on government contracts to observe employment conditions at least as good as those agreed in relevant collective agreements, a first attempt at government wage regulation favouring unions. In 1893 the Railway Regulation Act restricted working hours on the railways, while 1897 saw the Workmen's Compensation Act, a provision copied from Germany which for the first time gave employees a prescriptive right to medical expenses for industrial injuries.

At roughly the same time, incidentally, employers began to organise more formally to negotiate with unions at a national rather than local level. This had the advantage of taking some of the heat out of disputes between increasingly powerful unions and individual employers, and also – by setting wage rates across an industry or sector – tending to protect against low-cost new entrants (Demougin et al. 2019).

For example, in 1896, the Employers' Federation of Engineering Associations was set up, and shortly became involved in a lengthy dispute with engineering workers, which led to a lockout[9] by the employers in 1897. The

8 Later Resolutions were passed in 1909 and 1946, before repeal in the 1982 Employment Act.

9 A lockout occurs when an employer or group of employers suspends work, closes places of employment and refuses to provide employment unless workers agree to the terms proposed. Lockouts have been relatively rare in British industrial relations.

following year, a number of employers' organisations set up an Employers Parliamentary Council to counteract the influence of the TUC.[10] So the late Victorian years were gradually reshaping the relationship between employees and employers.

The early twentieth century

The years leading up to World War I were to be marked by increased industrial unrest and growing union power. But the new century had begun with a major setback to organised labour in the form of the Taff Vale judgment, a key element in the demonology of British industrial relations.

In 1900 the Amalgamated Society of Railway Servants[11] went on strike against the Taff Vale Railway company, seeking higher wages and union recognition. The company rapidly defeated the strike by importing strikebreakers from outside, but it pressed on with legal action against the union. The claim was that the picketing which occurred violated the Conspiracy and Protection of Property Act of 1875, and damages were sought.

The company won its case and was awarded £23,000 in damages and costs, the equivalent of nearly £4 million today. The union claimed that, as it was not a legal corporation, it could not be sued. It appealed and won, but then

---

10 Although the Council had some initial influence in and around the Taff Vale case, it did not become a permanent feature of the industrial relations landscape.

11 This became part of the National Union of Railwaymen, now merged into the National Union of Rail, Maritime and Transport Workers (the RMT).

in 1901, the House of Lords upheld the original verdict. The view was that, if unions could hold property and pay agents, as they now clearly could, then they were, by the same token, liable for damages if their acts caused financial and other costs to other parties. Their precise legal status was surely an irrelevance.

The effect on unions was stunning. The verdict meant that, in effect, although the 1870s' legislation had freed unions from the threat of criminal prosecution, they were still liable for civil action. Every time workers went on strike, their funds (in many cases tied up in friendly society welfare commitments) were now at risk. Though few employers took immediate advantage of the ruling, it was clear to the unions that it had to be reversed.

Despite the early association of trade unions with the Liberal Party,[12] dissatisfaction with the party's attitude towards unionism had already led to the formation of the Independent Labour Party in 1893, and the Labour Representation Committee (LRC) in 1900. Following the Taff Vale judgment, this movement towards a distinct Labour identity in Parliament was accelerated. At the 1906 General Election, LRC candidates won 29 seats (out of a possible 670). These new MPs were a factor in stiffening the resolve of Henry Campbell-Bannerman's Liberal government to produce the definitive legislation – the Trade Disputes Act of 1906 – which was to give the unions blanket immunity from civil action for breach of contract.

---

12 The first trade unionist standing as a 'Lib-Lab' candidate was former shoemaker George Odger, in a by-election as early as 1870.

Although there have been various subsequent modifications to the 1906 Act, this immunity endures today, and is what gives unions much of their power and influence. It was this act, remember, that Hayek was to see as the root of Britain's post-war industrial relations problems more than seventy years later.

But as Brodie (2003: 88) puts it, both the Royal Commission[13] set up following Taff Vale and the Trade Disputes Act 1906 were simply 'exercises in problem-solving'. This was adhockery, a fudge. No formal 'right to strike', such as is found in many other countries, was created. There was no attempt to make collective agreements legally enforceable, or to systematise collective bargaining. For instance, there were to be few procedural restraints on taking industrial action until the introduction of formal ballots in the 1980s. This was a situation which, paradoxically, while giving union officers a perhaps excessive degree of power, at the same time could be seen as an invitation to unofficial action.

As Phelps Brown (1983: 51) points out, the Trade Disputes Act meant that 'Parliament decided that, uniquely among all our institutions and procedures, trade unions and industrial relations should be exempt from regulation by law'. This principle of 'voluntarism' – that the state had no business interfering in collective bargaining – was to become an orthodoxy for many years and still has resonance today.

---

13 This one was the Royal Commission on Trade Disputes and Trade Combinations.

The emergence of a Parliamentary Labour Party was not universally welcomed by trade unionists,[14] and Liberal supporter Walter Osborne, of the Amalgamated Society of Railway Servants, brought a case against his union for using a political levy to support it (Moher 2009). Although his initial case failed, the House of Lords upheld his action in 1909. The Osborne judgement proved nearly as controversial as the Taff Vale verdict, but was eventually reversed by the Trade Union Act 1913. This Act legalised the political levy, but required unions to ballot their members to ratify funding, and to allow individuals to opt out of contributions. Although the rules were tightened under the Thatcher government of the 1980s, this remains the case today.

Parliamentary activity took place against a background of rising union militancy. Membership doubled from 2 million in 1905 to more than 4 million at the outbreak of World War I in 1914. From 1911 to 1914, there were more than 3,000 strikes – over 1,200 of these in 1913 alone. This period unsurprisingly became known as the 'Great Unrest'.

Although many industries were affected, most action was to be found among semi-skilled coal miners, textile workers, dock and transport workers. Much of this action was on a national scale. For example, 1911 saw the first nationwide railway workers' strike, while in the same year,

14 Other parties also made a play for support from trade unionists. For example, Andrew Bonar Law, later the Conservative Prime Minister, supported the Osborne judgement but favoured the payment of MPs, so that the influence of unions on Labour members 'would be destroyed' (Wrigley 2009: 63).

the National Sailors' and Firemen's Union was able to co-ordinate action in many port cities around the country. In the following year the miners' strike became the first to close pits across the country.

As so often in our economic history, the proximate force behind all this militancy seems to have been falling real wages. However, many union activists were also strongly influenced by syndicalist thinking during this period – the strategy being to build union confederations to weaken and eventually dispossess capitalist employers and for the workers subsequently to run industries.

Syndicalism, an import from the French labour movement, was influential in mining and transport, and was associated with the formation in early 1914 of the Triple Alliance of the Miners Federation of Great Britain, the National Union of Railwaymen, and the National Transport Workers Federation (which covered dockers, seamen, tramworkers and road vehicle workers). This alliance seemed to threaten an unprecedented level of joint action, but this was forestalled by the start of the Great War in August of the same year.

World War I

By the end of that month, the Labour Party and the TUC had declared an industrial truce for the duration of the war. Subsequently, three Labour MPs with union backgrounds – Arthur Henderson, George Barnes and John Hodge – were to become ministers in the Coalition government which Herbert Asquith formed in 1915.

During the hostilities, the state took previously unknown powers, including the ability to mobilise and direct labour. Military conscription was not introduced until 1916, but from the beginning of the war there was a need to control the expansion of the volunteer army so that necessary production should not be stripped of key workers. A National Register was established, with groups of key workers being held back from military service.

Some are said to have thought that the war would be over by Christmas, but this was soon proved illusory. The government began to use its new powers to allocate workers to jobs across the economy. Voluntary movements between jobs were controlled. Powers were taken to control wage increases, and two 'Treasury Agreements' were negotiated with unions to abandon strike action, relax restrictive practices and allow 'dilution' of skilled jobs in the war industries by employing unskilled men, and increasingly women, in these roles. Later, a new Ministry of Labour was created to bring together some of the pre-war functions which had been unsystematically accumulated by the Home Office, the Board of Trade and the Local Government Board (Parker 1957: 15). The first minister in charge was Labour MP John Hodge, formerly a trade union organiser.

Neither official union agreement to suspend normal industrial action, nor legal sanctions, however, were able to prevent unrest. Unionists demanding action ignored their leaders, taking matters into their own hands. Large-scale unofficial action by workers in Clydeside munitions factories in 1915 was echoed to a lesser degree in other urban industrial settings. A legacy of this wartime militancy was the creation in many industries of regular shop stewards[15] committees, which were to complicate industrial relations for decades to come.

Nevertheless, World War I saw a major increase in union recognition and national-level collective bargaining, with industry employers' associations taking a growing role. There was also high-level consultation between government and the TUC, and government-sponsored industry-level meetings between employers and unions in Whitley Councils[16] (Wrigley 2007: 207–8). This was coupled with a surge in union membership, including in areas such as agriculture and clothing where unionisation had been weak before the war (Wrigley 2015). The unions were no longer outsiders.

The inter-war years

Many government powers were relinquished at the end of the war, but precedents had been set which would be built on for much of the remainder of the twentieth century. An early peacetime development, for example, was the

---

15 There is no exact definition of a shop steward, but he or she is an elected representative of employees at the workplace. They are lay officials, and are thus not employed by the union, although they may nowadays have some part of their working time allocated to union duties under a 'facilities agreement' with the employer.

16 Joint Industrial Councils operating at national, district and workplace levels, they were intended to arbitrate between workers and employers. They spread after World War I, but later went into decline. A national Whitley Council still survives, however, in the Civil Service. The councils were named after J. H. Whitley, a Liberal MP whose committee recommended their introduction.

Industrial Courts Act of 1919. This gave governments the permanent ability to arbitrate in industrial disputes, subject to both parties agreeing (Brodie 2003: 166–68). These powers were to be used many times in the years to come.[17]

Another early post-war development was the formation of the International Labour Organization (ILO) as part of the League of Nations, set up under the 1919 Treaty of Versailles. Although UK officials and trade unionists were involved in the setting-up of the ILO – which worked from a British draft – this country stood aloof from its operation for many years, preferring to rely on voluntary arrangements rather than legislation on employment and collective bargaining to ratify ILO conventions.[18]

The return of peace at the end of 1918 saw renewed industrial militancy. Union membership had doubled during the war years, peaking at over 8 million members in 1920 (see Figure 4). This even spread to the police: there were police strikes in Liverpool and London in 1918 and 1919.[19] In 1919, the Clyde Workers Committee and the Scottish TUC's call for a 40-hour strike led to violence and troops being called in. The next year, dockers blocked the loading of arms intended for use in an abortive attempt to crush

---

17 In 1940 the government took the authority to make arbitration compulsory, and continued this power into the late 1950s (Frank 1959; Beaumont 1982).

18 Although the UK is nowadays signed up to the eight Fundamental Conventions (such as those banning forced labour and child employment, or mandating equal pay and the right to join a union), these are open to interpretation by UK courts. And there are many Conventions agreed by the ILO to which the UK is not signed up.

19 Leading to the Police Act 1919, which banned strike action, a ban which continues today.

the Russian October Revolution, an indication of the wider socialist objectives of some unionists in this period.

Figure 4   Trade union membership levels (thousands) 1892–1940

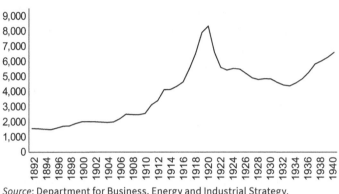

Source: Department for Business, Energy and Industrial Strategy.

The financial stringency of the immediate post-war years saw attempts to cut wages in both public and private sectors. In the coal-mining industry, which had been under government control during the war but had now been returned to its private owners, attempts to cut pay in the face of falling international demand precipitated a major strike in 1921. This might have been expected to trigger sympathetic action from the other members of the Triple Alliance, but this failed to materialise – a source of recrimination for years afterwards. On 'Black Friday' (15 April), the transport and rail unions announced that they were not going to strike. The miners struck alone, and were soon forced back to work.

The problems of the mining industry continued over the next few years. When Chancellor of the Exchequer Winston

Churchill returned Britain to the Gold Standard (Jenkins 1998: 307–10) in April 1925, this increased the pressure on costs and prompted the mine owners to demand pay cuts and longer hours. A temporary government subsidy was introduced to allow negotiations to continue, and to enable Sir Herbert Samuel to chair a rapid Royal Commission on the mining industry (Edgerton 2019: 184). But when the subsidy ended and Samuel recommended pay cuts, the miners refused to accept this, and the employers locked them out. The TUC consequently called a strike in May 1926 to support the miners.

This may have gone down to posterity as 'the General Strike', but the TUC only called out 2.5 million unionists (including the miners), around 15% of employed workers.[20] They faced a government which had prepared in advance and was able, with the assistance of many middle-class volunteers, to maintain emergency movement of supplies and skeleton services. The Labour Party, seeking to establish its electoral appeal as moderate and trustworthy, held back; its leader, Ramsay MacDonald, confided to his diary that the election of 'this fool', the militant miners' leader, Arthur Cook, looked like 'the most calamitous thing that has ever happened to the TU movement' (Wrigley 2009: 67).[21]

---

20 The TUC called out unionists on the railways, dockers, road transport workers, printers, iron and steel workers, and those working in metals, building, electricity and gas. After eight days, only a day before the strike was ended, engineers and shipbuilders were called out.

21 As Wrigley notes, MacDonald's sentiments towards Cook were probably similar to those felt by Neil Kinnock in relation to Arthur Scargill nearly sixty years later.

The TUC held discussions with Samuel and recommended a compromise, but the miners wouldn't agree. After just nine days, the General Council of the TUC called the strike off, some members apparently fearing that significant numbers were returning to work and support was crumbling (Morris 1976: ch. 4). The miners were alone again. They were eventually forced back to work in November, obliged to accept the owners' terms. This defeat created a bitterness which lasted into nationalisation and beyond: the collective memory of this period was often recalled by militant unionists in the very different conditions of the post-war years.

This was a disaster for the miners, but also a major setback for both the TUC and the broader labour movement. Employers used the opportunity to victimise striking workers; for example, nearly a quarter of the National Union of Railwaymen's membership were refused a return to work (Edgerton 2019: 85). Union membership, which had already fallen back from its 1920 peak of 8.3 million (45.2% of the employed workforce), continued a decline to the mid 1930s when it stood at only 4.6 million (23.5%).[22] Strike activity collapsed to very low levels after the heights of 1926 (Figure 5). The TUC turned to moderation, and an emphasis on cooperation with the Labour Party and parliamentary politics rather than concerted strike action.

---

22 It had recovered to 6.3 million (31.6%) by the outbreak of war in 1939. Fluctuations in total membership reflected shifts in demand during the inter-war period, with the decline of old industries and the rise of new types of manufacturing and services in different parts of the country, rather than being simply related to disillusion with unions.

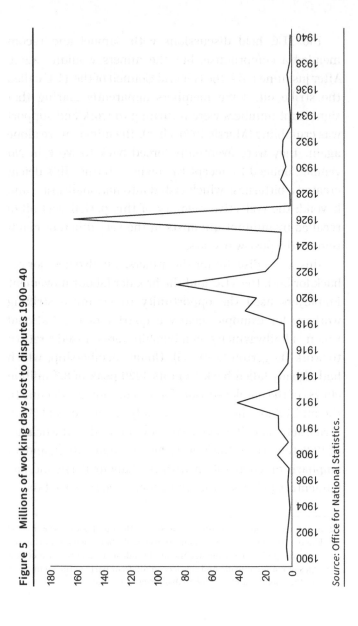

Figure 5 Millions of working days lost to disputes 1900–40

Source: Office for National Statistics.

This moderation was in part a response to the changes in the law associated with the 1927 Trade Disputes and Trade Union Act. The legislation in effect outlawed general and sympathetic strikes, which could incur both criminal and civil penalties. The immunities consequent on the 1871 and 1906 legislation were now to be applicable only to 'a trade dispute within a trade or industry in which the strikers were engaged' (Brodie 2003: 192). The Act also required unions to get members to 'contract in' to political levies, and banned civil servants and local government workers from joining unions affiliated to the TUC.

The TUC's new turn involved taking part in the Mond–Turner[23] talks, a series of discussions on industrial issues between unionists and employers which floated the idea of a National Industrial Council. This would have been a permanent forum for the 'two sides of industry' to discuss a wide range of issues, investigate problems, and set up conciliation procedures (Phelps Brown 1983: 122–25). As a result of the reluctance of employers' organisations, the talks ultimately achieved little (although they can be seen as a distant forerunner of the National Economic Development Council set up under Harold Macmillan in the early 1960s). The TUC also began to flirt with Keynesianism and pressed for public spending increases to combat unemployment – and later for rearmament in response to the growing menace of continental Fascism (Booth 1995: 22).

---

23 Sir Alfred Mond was chairman of Imperial Chemical Industries (ICI) and Ben Turner was the TUC president.

The economic recovery in the later 1930s saw union membership rising again. And this period also saw improvements to unemployment insurance and other benefits, while the Factories Act of 1937 made significant improvements to health and safety at work, and the Holidays with Pay Act, pushed by the TUC, extended the possibility of paid holidays to many workers.[24]

The first 150 years of trade unionism in this country constituted a turbulent period in which an initially weak labour movement, with little power and facing frequent employer intransigence and a harsh legal environment, gradually became an established feature of UK civil society as well as its economic structure.

While weakened by the collapse of the general strike, unions now had embedded immunity from criminal or civil action so long as industrial action stayed within reasonable bounds. World War II and the early post-war years were to see union power and influence increase far beyond the dreams of the early pioneers of unionism. This turned out, however, to be problematic for the country as a whole.

---

24 This Act did not give a right to paid holidays, but allowed Trade Boards (which had been set up under the Liberal government before World War I to cover 'sweated', low-paid industries) to make an award of one week's paid holiday (Brodie 2003: 210-11).

3 INDUSTRIAL RELATIONS IN POST-WAR BRITAIN

The 1939–45 conflict saw government intervention in the labour market reaching new heights. In 1940, under the Conditions of Employment and National Arbitration Order (Parker 1957: 448–57), strikes and lockouts were made illegal for the duration of the war, and binding arbitration was imposed where necessary – although normal collective bargaining continued, after a fashion. 'Manpower' planning covered much of the adult female, as well as male, population, however. Under the Registration for Employment Order 1941, women could be required to register in order to ascertain their availability for work to support the war effort. And the state took powers to amalgamate or close businesses in the interest of directing labour to wartime priorities.

Trade unions were given what amounted to a considerably elevated status in return for cooperation with such wartime measures as wage restraint and acquiescence to the direction of labour. They were, for instance, involved in consultation processes at the plant level in attempts to increase efficiency.

One of the most able union leaders of the inter-war years, Ernest Bevin of the Transport and General Workers

Union, became Minister of Labour and National Service.[1] As the standing and reputation of the unions increased, so did membership – which rose back to nearly 8 million again by the end of the war.

Unions were given greater clout by extending the scope of state regulation of low pay through the coalition's Wages Council[2] Act 1945, while the new Labour government quickly repealed the 1927 Trade Disputes and Trade Unions Act and passed a new Fair Wages Resolution in 1946.[3] It further entrenched the trade union movement in national life by placing people with a union background on the boards of the new nationalised industries, the BBC, official enquiries and commissions, and in the House of Lords.

Meanwhile, the financial difficulties of the early post-war years meant that there was a need to keep inflation low to prevent pressure on sterling in that time of rigidly fixed exchange rates. A White Paper in 1948 argued for wages to be held down and a period of pay restraint lasted until the surge in prices during the Korean War made it impossible

---

1   Bevin was a fierce anti-Communist – which fitted him well as Foreign Secretary in the early Cold War years – and an advocate of parliamentary socialism who was reluctant to use the strike weapon to pursue union objectives.

2   'Wages Councils' was the new name for the Trade Boards. From covering just four 'sweated trades' in 1909, these Boards covered 52 industries by 1938. They were a very early form of 'tripartism', with employer, union and government representation in the setting of pay and conditions.

3   Building on earlier such Resolutions, this was an administrative direction obliging the government to safeguard the employment standards of workers employed by firms on government contracts.

to sustain. This episode was, however, simply the first of a succession of more or less formal incomes policies which continued until the collapse of the Social Contract thirty years later.[4]

The voluntarist consensus and its problems

The partial incorporation of unions into the British estab-lishment was not challenged by the Conservatives when they returned to power in 1951. Far from it: at the 1947 Party Conference, Winston Churchill had declared that the 'trade unions are a long-established and essential part of our national life': they were 'pillars of our British Soci-ety'. He defended 'the right of individual labouring men to adjust their wages and conditions by collective bargain-ing, including the right to strike'. Although he had been a hawk during the General Strike and had previously been accused of excessive force against trade unionists when Home Secretary, Churchill was now more than concili-atory towards trade unionism. He returned to his theme at the 1950 Conference, urging 'every Tory craftsman or wage

---

4   Apart from Stafford Cripps's wage freeze of 1948–50, there were the Con-servatives' 'Pay Pause' in the early 1960s; Labour's voluntary policy in 1965, Harold Wilson's 1966 statutory policy freezing pay and then setting rigid 'norms' (accompanied by a National Board for Prices and Incomes which was scrapped by the Conservatives in 1970); the Conservatives' six-month freeze in 1972–73, followed by pay targets (and new institutions in a Pay Board and a Prices Commission); and Labour's Social Contract from 1975 to 1979. These initiatives usually had some brief initial effect in holding back pay increases, but soon collapsed as inflation was driven by increases in the money supply rather than independent union 'wage push'. See Brit-tan (1979).

earner' to be an active member of a trade union (Wrigley 2009: 69).

This benign attitude towards the unions was continued by Churchill's successors, Anthony Eden and Harold Macmillan. Even when a scandal emerged in the Electrical Trades Union in 1961, with allegations of Communist ballot-rigging (Dorey 2009: 123),

> [v]oluntarism once again prevailed, because there emerged a general acceptance by Ministers that it would be inappropriate for them to impose model rules on the trade unions. Any attempt to do so would be widely viewed by the trade unions as direct governmental interference in their internal affairs.

By the early 1960s, the legitimacy of unions in economic and social life was to be further enhanced by participation in a variety of 'tripartite' bodies (involving unions, employers and government). The most obvious example was the TUC's representation on the new National Economic Development Council, which discussed economic policy with a view towards 'indicative planning' on the French model.

The unions thus grew in power and influence over the 1950s and 1960s as membership grew and union density – the proportion of employees in unions – rose to about 45% and the coverage of collective bargaining a good deal higher.[5] However, this development was increasingly seen

---

5 Collective bargaining typically determines pay for all workers in a category, not just those who are union members.

as holding back productivity growth which, though arguably more than respectable by historical standards, was lagging behind that in other Western European countries.

There was much discussion of 'restrictive practices', by which unions attempted to influence staffing levels, training and apprenticeships, the pace of production and the introduction of new equipment and methods of working. One particular bugbear was demarcation disputes, occasioned by the high degree of multiunionism in Britain as a result of its long history of union development. Despite the 1939 TUC-brokered Bridlington Agreement, this feature of the British industrial relations scene led to recurrent inter-union disputes about who should do what, breaking out afresh whenever management wished to introduce new machinery or rearrange work practices.[6]

A further problem lay in the UK's two-tier system of industrial relations, with the initiative often lying with the powerful shop stewards movement at the level of the factory or other workplace. Between 1960 and 1979 over 90% of strikes and other industrial action (such as overtime bans and working to rule) began unofficially (Metcalf 1993: 273). National union leaders were often obliged to acquiesce in making strikes official, even if their own inclination would have been against the action.

It has been estimated that there were around 150,000 shop stewards in the early 1960s, out of a total union

---

6   This was a situation avoided in West Germany, where the post-war recasting of industrial relations after the Nazi period (ironically assisted by advice from UK unionists) had led to a small number of industry-based unions.

membership of around 9.5 million (Kynaston 2014: 147). Such a large number of local representatives sometimes made it difficult for union executives to devise a consistent and effective strategy.

There was also a different set of concerns about how union power could oppress individuals. A major issue was the closed shop, an agreement often acquiesced in by management in order to avoid inter-union disputes, whereby all employees in a given category had to belong to a particular union.

In a famous case (*Rookes v Barnard*) in the early 1960s, a draughtsman at the British Overseas Airways Corporation (BOAC) left his union, the Association of Engineering and Shipbuilding Draughtsmen, after a disagreement. The union then threatened to strike unless BOAC sacked him. When they first suspended and then dismissed him, Douglas Rookes sued the union officials, including branch chairman Mr Barnard. After a long legal battle, the House of Lords found in favour of Mr Rookes. This verdict outraged the unions, and its effect was reversed by the incoming Labour government passing the Trade Disputes Act 1965.

Concern over issues such as these led Harold Wilson's administration to set up a Royal Commission on Trade Unions and Employers Associations under Lord Donovan, a distinguished lawyer. Reporting in June 1968 following three years of deliberation, Donovan was strongly influenced by the 'Oxford School' of industrial relations academics, most notably Hugh Clegg and Otto Kahn-Freund, who rejected the view that there should be major changes in the law.

Clegg and Kahn-Freund were long-time champions of voluntarism (Flanders 1974), dating back, as we have seen, to the late nineteenth century. The view was that employers and unions should be left to determine appropriate pay and working conditions via free collective bargaining (or 'joint regulation'[7]) without state intervention.[8] Strikes were unfortunate, but legalistic reforms would achieve nothing. For example, if employers were given back the freedom to sue unions for breach of contract, as Hayek would have wanted, it was argued that they would not use it (Phelps Brown 1983: 184). There were recommendations for some minor legislative changes, such as protection against 'unfair' dismissal and a provision that employers should not be able to include no-union clauses in contracts. But the main hope for improved industrial relations was placed on reducing unofficial strikes by reforming union structures, encouraging collective bargaining by appointing more full-time officials and improved training of shop stewards, and promoting productivity agreements. None of this required new laws.

Harold Wilson found Donovan's conclusions underwhelming. He, and his government, had been badly bruised in the 1966 strike by the National Union of Seamen. That

---

7   Allan Flanders (1968) pointed out that unions didn't really 'bargain' as they were not a contracting party. They simply negotiated with management the rules on which pay bargains were set. This is one reason why governments have resisted making pay agreements legally enforceable, though the reasoning is tenuous.

8   Clegg held that both employers and unions had legitimate, but clearly distinct, functions: he was opposed to worker participation in management and saw unions as playing a permanent oppositional role in a pluralist 'industrial democracy' (Clegg 1960; Ackers 2007).

strike had caused great disruption to shipping and trade, damaged the balance of payments, caused a run on the pound, and undermined the government's attempt to hold down wage increases. Wilson alleged at the time that the strike had been taken over by communists aiming to bring down his government (Pimlott 1992: 405–8). He was keen to take steps to prevent damaging strikes of this kind. At the beginning of 1969, his combative Secretary of State, Barbara Castle, published her optimistically titled White Paper 'In Place of Strife'. The aim was to regulate union behaviour by giving the Employment Secretary the power to require pre-strike ballots, mandate conciliation pauses, and to impose settlements on unofficial inter-union disputes. The paper also proposed setting up a body which could impose fines for breaches of rules.

By the standards of later industrial relations reforms, these proposals were modest. The public liked them; even a majority of Labour voters were in favour (Sandbrook 2006: 711). Nevertheless, they were too much for the unions and many members of Wilson's cabinet, most notably Home Secretary James Callaghan, a wily operator who used his opposition to build up support within the union movement with an eye to eventually becoming Prime Minister. Despite Wilson's determination to push through reform, he was eventually forced to back down and accept a 'solemn and binding' agreement by union leaders and the TUC to use their influence to reduce strikes, especially unofficial ones (Pimlott 1992: 528–44). This agreement had some influence for a short time in reducing unofficial action, but this did not last. Wider concerns about union power were not assuaged.

When the Conservatives under Edward Heath returned to government in 1970, they were determined to take a tougher line than Wilson, particularly as the number of strikes and working days lost had continued to rise despite the promises made by the unions when Barbara Castle's proposed reforms were dropped.

Consequently, Heath's administration introduced the 1971 Industrial Relations Act, which established legally enforceable collective bargaining, compulsory pre-strike ballots and a conciliation pause before any strike which might threaten the national interest. A National Industrial Relations Court (NIRC) was set up. This was intended to settle industrial disputes and define and proscribe 'unfair' industrial practices. The pre-entry closed shop (where workers had to join unions before being employed) was abolished, although a version of this arrangement (the 'agency shop'[9]) could be maintained by a ballot.

Unfortunately for the Heath government, despite public opinion again broadly supporting reform, the new legislation was fiercely resisted by unions, some members of which refused point-blank to accept it. In one famous incident in 1972, the President of the NIRC, Sir John Donaldson, jailed five dockers (the 'Pentonville Five') for breaching an injunction against picketing. This brought the bulk of the country's 42,000 dockers out on strike. They were soon joined by large numbers of unofficial sympathy strikers – car workers, bus drivers, printers, building workers and many others – and

---

9   In an agency shop workers would not have to be members of the union, or bound by its decisions, but would have to pay a fee towards the cost of organising collective bargaining.

the TUC planned to call a one-day strike. The House of Lords, still at that time the ultimate legal authority, conveniently found that the imprisoned men had been acting as agents of their union and therefore could not be held personally liable. Hours later, they were freed.

It was not only unionists who were unhappy with the Industrial Relations Act. The Act was complicated, and many employers did not want to get bogged down in legal proceedings. As the Donovan Commission's reasoning had suggested, few applied to the NIRC for remedy in relation to unfair industrial practices, and after the Pentonville Five case this facility was effectively ignored. Many employers preferred to deal with unions and resolve issues themselves rather than bring in the lawyers. Some may have quite happily accepted arrangements such as the single-union closed shop as they felt this made industrial relations simpler.

The new legislation had done very little to reduce strikes.[10] With rising inflation (Figure 6) associated with rapid monetary expansion under Heath's Chancellor of the Exchequer Anthony Barber, and later the effect of the OPEC oil price hike, the unions were in no mood for moderation. Working days lost to strikes rose to a then post-war high of nearly 24 million in 1972. A lengthy miners' strike that year saw mass picketing preventing coal supplies getting to power stations, giving the miners victory as power cuts loomed. An imposed freeze on wages and prices at the end of the year added to the febrile atmosphere.

---

10 During the less than four years of Heath's government, no fewer than five States of Emergency were declared as a result of strike action, an extraordinary number of occasions in so short a period. Since 1974, no such declarations have been made: even during the pandemic, these powers were not deployed.

Figure 6   Post-war inflation: Retail Price Index All Items percentage change over 12 months (January 1987 = 100)

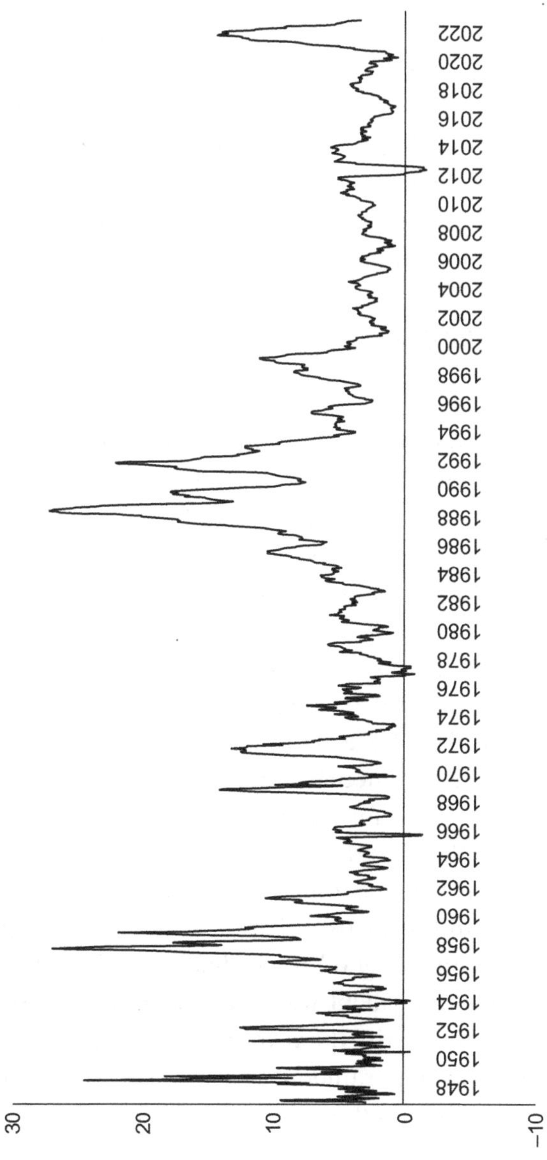

Source: ONS (2024).

In 1973, the miners voted for further strike action, leading Heath to impose a three-day week at the end of the year to conserve energy supplies. In the February 1974 'who rules Britain?' general election, Heath sought a mandate for yet tougher action against the unions, but a surge in Liberal Party votes led to the Conservatives being defeated and Labour coming back into government.

The Social Contract and the Winter of Discontent

The Labour Party did not, however, have a majority of seats in the House of Commons, and so Harold Wilson called another election in October of the same year. British electors seem to dislike being asked to vote too frequently, and the second election only marginally improved the government's position, giving it an overall majority of just three seats – a majority which it was soon to lose as James Callaghan replaced Wilson as Prime Minister in April 1976. Later that same year, the desperate state of the UK economy led to Callaghan's Chancellor Denis Healey famously having to go to the International Monetary Fund for a record $3.9 billion loan in a bid to shore up the pound.

Labour had economic problems throughout its period of office in the 1970s. Inflation remained high, following the 1973 and 1979 oil price shocks, as did interest rates, while unemployment was at levels not previously seen in the post-war years. The government's relationship with the unions was of paramount importance during this period. Harold Wilson had repealed the Conservatives' Industrial

Relations Act early on, passing Labour's own Trade Union and Labour Relations Act in 1974 to restore the unions' position to that before the 1971 Act. In return for union agreement to a voluntary incomes policy – grandly known as the 'Social Contract' – the government passed further legislation to extend individual and union 'rights'. The Employment Protection Act 1975 made it more difficult to dismiss workers, and enabled unions to obtain statutory recognition through ACAS, the government's Advisory, Conciliation and Arbitration Service.[11]

This period was the apogee of union visibility, power and influence. Union membership rose sharply, as Figure 7 indicates, and the number of shop stewards rose in line, to more than 300,000 by 1979. Closed-shop agreements proliferated, covering 5 million workers by the end of the decade.

Figure 7   Trade union membership levels (thousands) 1940–2020

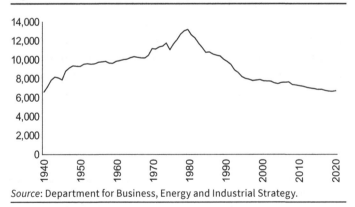

Source: Department for Business, Energy and Industrial Strategy.

---

11 Since rebranded, twenty-first-century style, as acas.

Management, attempting to improve industrial relations, increasingly assisted the process of unionisation by deducting union dues from salaries, which gave unions a regular flow of income without the trouble and costs of collecting it. Because an incomes policy was in operation, however, questions about bargaining away restrictive practices were deferred or forgotten. 'Big Beast' union leaders were constantly in the news; in 1977 Jack Jones, general secretary of the Transport and General Workers Union, was voted by 54% in one Gallup poll to be the most powerful man in Britain.

But although the leaders of the main unions, albeit with different degrees of enthusiasm, supported the Social Contract, activist shop stewards took a different line and the wished-for improvement in industrial relations failed to appear. Far from it: there were occasions, such as during the long-running Grunwick dispute,[12] when scenes of mass picketing and violent clashes between activists and the police provoked fears of anarchy. Inflation was a constant problem, and militants pressed for higher and higher pay increases to compensate for and outrun it. Post-war record levels of strikes and days lost occurred, culminating in the 'Winter of Discontent' of 1978–79 when, according to Dominic Sandbrook's (2013: 758) graphic account,

---

12 Grunwick was a photograph processing company which employed many Asian workers, whose dispute became a cause célèbre with the Left. The picket line attracted large numbers of unionists from all over the country, including Arthur Scargill of the National Union of Mineworkers and prominent ministers including Shirley Williams. See Sandbrook (2013: 599–618) for an account.

this was a crisis that saw ports, schools and railway stations shut down, businesses starved of essential supplies,
farmers forced to slaughter their livestock for lack of
fodder and thousands of workers defying not just their
government but their own representatives ... The sick
genuinely went untreated; the dead did go unburied.

Of course, this was hardly the end of civilisation as we knew
it, and even with all these strikes, most people were working
normally and able to go about their business. But constant
industrial disruption clearly had an impact on public opinion, and the polls increasingly turned against Callaghan's
government. The prime minister and his cabinet were vis-
ibly tiring of the struggle, and it was no great surprise when
the general election of May 1979 returned the Conservatives,
now under Margaret Thatcher's leadership, to office.

The Thatcher–Major reforms and after

The events of the later 1970s meant that the Conservatives
had no option but to return to the task of trade union reform. They could scarcely ignore it, as strikes continued
to come thick and fast: there were several new disputes
and considerably more days lost in the second half of 1979,
after the Conservatives took over, than in the first part of
the year (Edgerton 2019: 410).

This time, however, the frontal approach adopted
by the Heath administration was abjured in favour of a
more pragmatic, gradualist programme. Over the period
1980–93 there were eight significant pieces of legislation

by which the legal and institutionalist basis of industrial relations was to be transformed step by step.

Despite this gradualism, the Thatcher administration is still probably best-remembered on the domestic front for taking on, and defeating, the striking miners led by Arthur Scargill.[13] There is no doubt that this victory, costly though it may have been in terms of social discord, was a key element in tackling the excessive power of the trade unions, which had built up in the 1960s and 1970s.

In 1981 the government faced a number of industrial relations challenges, including a major civil service dispute, and had backed down when faced with the threat of another miners' strike. But plans were then laid to build up huge stocks of coal, which would enable the National Coal Board and the government to hold out for many months without any danger of the power cuts that had done for the Heath administration, while also organising a national police response to face down intimidating mass picketing.

The year 1984 was crucial. On 25 January it was announced that trade unions would be banned at Government Communications Headquarters (GCHQ), the intelligence and signals research station at Cheltenham. This was Mrs Thatcher's response to concerns about security which had been raised during the Winter of Discontent and then again in the 1981 civil service strike when one union officer threatened to hit GCHQ hard with militant

---

13 Almost 40 years on, the miners' strike still casts a long shadow over UK politics today. *The Guardian*, 27 August 2023 (https://www.theguardian.com/commentisfree/2023/aug/27/40-years-miners-strike-long-shadow-uk-politics-pit-closures).

action. A final straw was the arrest of a GCHQ official for sexual offences and the subsequent revelation that he had been selling secrets to the Soviet Union. While not directly related to union action, the case brought unwanted publicity and confirmed the prime minister's distaste for 'the enemy within' such a sensitive organisation (see Moore 2015: 136–42).[14] The GCHQ ban was to arouse considerable union anger and legal challenges.

A few weeks later, in early March, the fateful miners' strike began. This dispute, which lasted for more than a year and ended with the defeat of the miners, has entered the realm of legend.[15] The details of the ebb and flow of this conflict are covered in the second volume of Charles Moore's biography of Margaret Thatcher (Moore 2015: 142–82). It is probably more important here to look at the broader picture of the Conservatives' reforms, which fundamentally reshaped British trade unionism.

New legislation was presented at roughly two-yearly intervals, with each stage being presented as a logical follow-up to earlier measures, or as a response to further union intransigence (for example, in the miners' strike). Particular concerns, such as the closed shop, were revisited more than once. The process continued even after

---

14 GCHQ's position was perhaps anomalous as union membership was already banned at SIS and MI5, two other key state security organisations. The GCHQ ban was eventually revoked when Labour returned to power in 1997, in exchange for a no-strike agreement.

15 In chapter 13 of *The Downing Street Years* (Thatcher 1993) – 'Mr Scargill's Insurrection' – Mrs Thatcher herself presented an interesting chronicle of the strike. It suggests that the defeat of the National Union of Mineworkers was rather less inevitable than later accounts have painted it.

Mrs Thatcher herself had left the scene and John Major took over as prime minister. It was the result of careful planning: some details are set out in Table 1.

Table 1   The main elements of the Thatcher–Major industrial relations reforms

Employment Act 1980	Statutory recognition procedures abolished
	Grounds to refuse to join union extended
	Picketing away from own workplace unlawful
	Restrictions on secondary action
	Restrictions on closed shop
	Public funds available for secret ballots
Employment Act 1982	Fair Wages Resolution rescinded
	Closed shop further weakened
	Definition of trade dispute in which unions immune from tort actions narrowed
	Selective dismissal of strikers permitted in some circumstances
Trade Union Act 1984	Secret ballots every five years for union executives
	Secret ballots prior to industrial action
	Secret ballots for political levy
Wages Act 1986	Wages Councils rates restricted
Employment Act 1988	Powers to grant injunctions to union members to prevent strikes going ahead
	Commissioner for Rights of Trade Union Members
	Rights of union members to inspect accounts
	Closed shop further weakened
	Separate strike ballots required for each workplace
Employment Act 1989	Restrictions on working time of women and youth lifted
	Exemption of small firms from some employment laws
	Rights to time off for union duties restricted

Employment Act 1990	Firms could selectively dismiss for unofficial action
	All secondary action outlawed
	Pre-entry closed shop abolished
	Union liability for unofficial action extended
Trade Union Reform and Employment Rights Act 1993	Tighter restrictions on strike ballots and union mergers
	More union accounting requirements
	Ballots for check-off arrangements
	Public funds for ballots phased out
	Abolition of Wages Councils

Source: Adapted from Shackleton (1998).

The first objective was the narrowing of legitimate union action in furtherance of a dispute. This entailed requiring formal, independently monitored, postal ballots prior to strikes. It also involved the end of coercive mass picketing of the kind seen in the 1970s in the miners' strikes of 1972 and 1974 and the Grunwick dispute, and which had its last hurrah in the miners' 'Battle of Orgreave' in June 1984. A related development was the ending of the grounds for secondary and sympathetic strike action; in future legitimate action could only be taken against your direct employer.

A second objective was to make unions financially responsible for torts committed by their members, thus forcing them to clamp down on the unofficial action which had been such a problem from the 1960s onwards.

Thirdly, government support for collective bargaining was severely scaled back. The ACAS-based union recognition route was closed and consultation rights in a number of areas were reduced. The scope of Wages Councils was at first cut back: they were eventually abolished, while the

Fair Wages Resolution (which, remember, required government contractors to pay best-practice rates) was scrapped. All these measures were aimed at cutting back the power and influence of trade unions, which had grown almost continuously since World War II.

A fourth objective was the restriction and eventual abolition in 1990 of the closed shop, the demise of which created less uproar than might have been expected. It had always been hard to justify on other than pragmatic grounds, and was out of tune with a changing society where people increasingly asserted personal freedoms.

A final recurrent theme was the reform of unions' own internal organisation and procedures. This uncharacteristic Conservative interference with private voluntary bodies was a decisive rejection of the industrial relations pieties of the early post-war decades. It was justified by the claim that undemocratic procedures had allowed unrepresentative militants too much influence: the Conservatives were giving back the unions to their members. Reforms included the requirement for regular secret ballots to elect and reelect officials and to support political levies, the right for individual members to see union accounts (it now seems extraordinary that members were ever denied this right) and to take legal action to restrain unions.

Since 1993, there have been few further legislative changes to the industrial relations environment. Despite having been hugely critical of many of the Conservatives' reforms, when Labour returned to power in 1997, they did not reverse them. Apart from the introduction of a renewed right for unions to apply for compulsory union recognition in 1998, there were few changes (Shackleton 2007: 457). Some minor gains for trade unions occurred following European Union directives, such as consultation over collective redundancies.

After the Conservatives came back (at first in coalition with the Liberal Democrats), there followed only some limited tweaks, such as the tightening of strike ballot rules in the Trade Union Act 2016, and giving employers the option to bring in agency workers on a temporary basis to replace strikers (which the courts later overruled).

Nevertheless, the last thirty years saw a dramatic reduction in the significance of the trade union movement in the UK, with a big fall in union membership (and a reduction in the number of unions, as is noted in the next chapter). The wave of strikes from mid 2022 may appear to be a break with this decline, but its longer-term significance remains to be seen.

4   UNIONISM TODAY

Any discussion of UK trade unions today, and of their prospects for the future, must start by attempting to explain the more or less continuous decline of the unionisation rate from a high point of 53% in 1980 to just 22.3% in 2022 (Figure 8). This decline has left a very different union movement from that which had been largely responsible for the defeat of the Heath and Callaghan governments in the 1970s, and which, as pointed out in the previous chapter, was to be fundamentally challenged by the Conservatives under Mrs Thatcher.

Why has unionisation declined?

What accounts for this decline? Clearly the legislative changes brought about by the Thatcher–Major governments had a considerable impact. Many on the Left see this as the key explanation and would like to see many of the laws listed in Table 1 repealed, in the belief that this would help reverse the downward trend. Perhaps it would, to some degree, but it is very doubtful that this alone would suffice. For the decline in union membership has many causes. Significantly, it is not confined to the UK. On the contrary, it is apparent in most

OECD countries, few of which have adopted industrial relations reforms of the kind we saw in the UK, and many of which have indeed positively encouraged unionisation through the European Union's emphasis on 'social partnership' between representatives of capital and labour (Visser 2023).

Figure 8   Trade union density (%) Great Britain 1980–2020

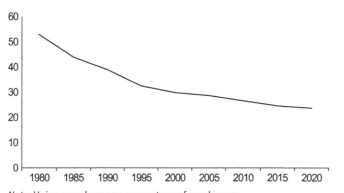

Note: Union members as a percentage of employees.
Source: 1980–90 from Booth (1995); 1995–2020 from BEIS.

Between 1980 and 2019, unionisation across the OECD fell from 36.5% to 15.8%. This is perhaps not comparing like with like, as there are more OECD countries today, particularly given the breakup of the Soviet bloc. A better comparison is shown in Figure 9, where union density has fallen since 2000 in virtually every country shown. This is true even in the Nordic countries,[1] which have

---

1   In Sweden, Finland and Denmark (and also in Iceland and Belgium), the main responsibility for unemployment benefits belongs with trade unions. As accessing these benefits requires union membership, this is a major reason for continuing high levels of unionisation in these countries.

traditionally had – and still have – very high levels of unionisation (Hogedahl et al. 2022).

Figure 9   Trade union density, selected countries 2000–19 (or latest available date)

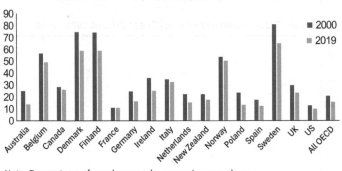

Note: Percentage of employees who are union members.
Source: OECD.

So what factors, other than changing legislation, account for declining union density? We need to concentrate rather more on the private sector, for that is where the decline has been sharpest. Between 1995 and 2022, union density in the public sector fell from 61.3% to 48.6%, but in the private sector, it fell from 26.3% to just 13%. Given that almost the entire remaining concentration of private sector union members is in ex–public sector entities such as Royal Mail and the utilities, union presence among other private businesses, especially new ones, is often very low or even nugatory.

A factor which has affected all developed countries is structural change associated with technological innovation, globalisation and changes in consumer tastes and preferences.

This has seen a shift from economies heavily dependent on manufacturing and extractive industries, where workers were concentrated in large-scale plants, often living close to their work, to more dispersed service businesses with little tradition of union presence. One UK study (Blanchflower and Bryson 2008) suggested that as much as a third of the decline in private sector union recognition between 1980 and 2004 was attributable to changes in workplace characteristics. This was not because unions were being derecognised in existing plants, but rather that new workplaces were not being unionised.[2]

Within sectors, there has also been a decline in union density, probably because unionised firms have grown less rapidly than non-unionised firms (see chapter 6). There has been a similar process in the US (Hirsch 2012: 136).

Associated with this has been a decline in national sectoral bargaining. Larger private businesses are often part of multinational corporations which prefer to organise their own pay levels and structures rather than be part of a national organisation. Sector-wide Employers' Associations, although they continue to exist, now play a far smaller role in the UK than they did for a large part of the twentieth century (Gooberman et al. 2019; Bryson and Willman 2022). In 1976, over 200 Employers Associations were recognised by the government's Certification Officer as taking part in collective bargaining; in March 2023 this number had fallen to just 38.

---

2   In a similar way, union membership has declined not so much because individuals have left unions (increased outflow) but rather that fewer people are entering union membership (reduced inflow) than in the past (Bryson et al. 2017).

This decline in the importance of sector-wide bargaining has also occurred in Germany (Günther and Höpner 2023), where large businesses now seem to favour greater wage competition rather than setting rates across the sector. Most other EU countries, however, have maintained national collective agreements.

The decentralisation of collective bargaining will probably have been a factor in reducing union bargaining strength. It will also have had the effect of increasing the costs of trade union organisation: bargaining with several different companies, rather than one employers' body, stretches resources. So too will have been the rise in the proportion of private sector employment in small (fewer than 50 employees) enterprises, now up to 48%. Recruitment and organisation has historically been more costly and difficult in smaller businesses, and as these businesses tend to have little market power, monopoly rents are not available to be snapped up by strong unions.

Added to this is the changing role and workload of union representatives in the British workplace. More – and more complicated – employment legislation, coupled with changing human resource management practices and greater diversity among employees, has increased the range and complexity of individual problems which officials and lay representatives are called upon to help with. As Bryson and Forth (2011: 263) point out, 'individual grievance representation has become increasingly important as a union servicing activity. This is particularly resource-intensive.'

Another long-run problem affecting union organisation in all countries may be what Willman et al. (2020), following Baumol (2012), refer to as the 'cost disease'. In Baumol's analysis, those sectors of the economy delivering personal services – for example, social and health care, education, and the performing arts – are unable by their nature to generate significant productivity gains. As the pay of workers in these areas must keep in touch with that of employees in other sectors, over time the cost of providing these services must logically tend to rise relative to goods and services where productivity gains are feasible. The claim is that recruiting and organising union members is a service of the kind to which Baumol refers.

Rising costs of organisation can be mitigated in various ways, such as placing greater reliance on unpaid local organisers rather than paid union officials or by reducing the costs of collecting dues via a 'check-off' system (Pyper 2018), if the employer can still be persuaded to deduct them directly from pay. The need to control costs leads to a concentration on groups of workers who are easiest to organise, while neglecting other potential members.

It is also an obvious motivation for union mergers. Between 1998 and 2020–21, the number of unions recognised by the Certification Officer fell from 238 to 133. By the latter date just seven unions, each with at least 250,000 members, accounted for almost three-quarters of total union membership. But union mergers, like mergers of companies, do not in themselves solve anything. While some merged unions strengthened and even grew their numbers, others did not. Unite, for example, was formed in 2007 by the merger of Amicus and the Transport and General Workers' Union and became the largest union in the UK at the time. By 2020, however, its numbers had fallen by more than 700,000, more than a third of its membership.[3]

To the extent that rising costs cannot be contained, union dues may rise, and this probably has at least a minor negative effect on the propensity to join unions. There is, as far as I know, no empirical evidence for the UK but, using Finnish data, Barth et al. (2020b) find a small but significant negative price-elasticity of demand, suggesting rising union dues may have some effect on union membership.

Alternatives to unionism

In addition to these cost issues, there is also the consideration that employees may now have available, in effect, 'substitutes' for union membership which were not available in the 1970s and 1980s. As Visser (2023: 9) puts it, in their current stage of decline, 'unions face competition from more technologically advanced and perhaps less costly solutions' to the problems workers have historically faced in their dealings with powerful employers. In Visser's view, functions which unions once provided in a package may now be available in other ways. Legal advice may be available cheaply on the internet; education, training and

---

3 Revealed: Unite Union has lost more than 700,000 members since it was formed. *Huffington Post*, 6 April 2022 (https://www.huffingtonpost.co.uk/entry/unite-union-membership-sharon-graham_uk_624b112ee4b007d3845958ba).

updating can be obtained more easily than in the past. In any case, the state is far more active in the labour market than thirty or forty years ago, and a wide range of regulation now protects workers and requires various employer-provided benefits which only the strongest unions seemed able to win in the past.

In earlier times, unions supported voluntarism and free collective bargaining. They were suspicious of state interventions which might undermine the rationale for joining unions. For example, they were largely opposed to a national minimum wage until the TUC, after a long campaign by General Secretary Rodney Bickerstaffe[4] and others, finally accepted the objective in 1986. Even then it was opposed by one of the largest unions, the Transport and General Workers Union (TGWU, later merged into Unite). Moreover, unionists were suspicious of European-style regulatory initiatives until European Commission President Jacques Delors made a famous speech to the TUC's 1988 conference at Bournemouth. Since then, however, the trade union movement has pressed for ever-increasing government intervention to promote new 'rights' for employees.

Governments have hugely expanded labour market regulation over the last thirty years. Some of this was in response to European initiatives while we were in the European Union, but it has mainly been home-grown – and pushed as much by the Conservatives as by the Labour Party (Shackleton 2017: 232–33). While unions

---

4   Peter Morris: National minimum wage. Rodney Bickerstaffe archives, 22 March 2020 (https://rodneybickerstaffe.org.uk/national-minumum-wage).

have supported and promoted this, they may have been undermining their own position, as the TGWU feared in the 1980s. For workers are now protected by minimum wages, unfair dismissal laws, anti-discrimination legislation and a proliferation of health and safety rules. We have ACAS dispute conciliation and employment tribunals[5] to tackle individual grievances. There are mandatory employer contributions to private pensions, parental leave and flexible working arrangements. As Forth and Bryson (2019) point out, low-paid workers in particular seem to have gained far more through government regulation than through collective bargaining, which makes union membership less attractive. Unions find it difficult to extend representation to those working short hours, particularly in the 'gig' economy, and those in small firms, especially when facing employers who may be hostile towards unionism (Gall 2021).

One argument for union activity, most often associated with Freeman and Medoff (1984: 8), is that of 'providing workers as a group with a means of communicating with management'. With such a facility, unionists can feel that they have a 'voice' at work, and their concerns will at least be discussed with employers and in some cases resolved.

It may be that such a voice can improve the match of pay and working conditions offered by management with

---

5 Employment tribunals began life as industrial tribunals in the mid 1960s, covering employer appeals related to training levies. They now adjudicate on issues such as unfair dismissal, discrimination, leave arrangements, flexible working, and many other labour matters. Where a full tribunal is held, one of the panel must normally be someone with a union background.

those sought by employees. For example, workers might prefer an employment offer which involves short hours and lower pay to long hours and higher pay. If the cost implications are neutral, workers could gain, and employers would be no worse off – indeed might actually gain if the union voice tended to reduce turnover and improve morale and productivity. Perhaps so – I will return to this later – but there are nowadays non-union means by which employees can have their say. The expansion of the human resource management function[6] within businesses has led to much greater formal emphasis on consultation and listening to employee concerns, while many large firms which operate within the EU continue, even post-Brexit, to have representation on European Works Councils for their UK workers.

Bryson et al. (2013), drawing on Workplace Employment Relations Survey data, show that there has been an expansion over time of management-led voice opportunities, with team briefings, regular meetings with management, problem-solving groups, and similar opportunities for consultation.

Given this, the need for union membership may seem much less obvious to new labour force entrants than was the case in the past. Union membership has in effect been 'crowded out' by government regulation and the expansion

---

6 The Chartered Institute of Personnel Development (CIPD), formerly the Institute of Personnel Management, has 160,000 members, up from 12,000 in 1979. The CIPD estimates that the 'people profession' now accounts for about 1.6% of the workforce: just under half a million people are employed in HR roles in the UK.

of the human resource management profession, at least in the private sector.[7]

All of this suggests that the causes of decline in unionisation are complex, and that it will not be reversed simply by repealing legislation which restricts union powers. Pushing water uphill is never easily achieved.

So who are union members?

Another observation is that today's workforce is much more diverse than in the heyday of UK trade unionism. For example, in the 1970s, female unionists were a smallish minority, and female trade union leaders more or less non-existent. Dominant groups such as miners, dockers, railway workers, shipyard workers, gas, telephone electricity and steelworkers were often close to 100% male. By contrast, today women are significantly more likely to be unionists than men: in 2022, union density among female employees was 25.6%, as against 19.1% for males. In some areas of union strength, such as education and health, women are three-quarters of employees.

---

7 In the public sector, though the same trends are discernible, the decline in membership has been less marked. Both in local and central government, and in the various agencies and quangos through which the state delivers many of its objectives, political pressure from allies in political parties and elsewhere continue to give unions more clout than might otherwise be expected. Whereas a pay increase which renders a private business no longer competitive will lead to job losses, pay increases in the public sector are largely passed on to the taxpayer as job losses are fiercely resisted by a hundred and one pressure groups.

Or take ethnic diversity. From their overwhelming dominance in the 1970s, white British workers are now only 78% of all those in work, and a smaller proportion of employees. Black or Black British workers are more likely to be in unions than other ethnicities, while Asian, Asian British and Chinese heritage employees are more rarely union members.

The greater diversity of the workforce may mean that different groups will have different priorities, and may join interest groups focusing on particular issues of importance to them – e.g. religion, sexuality, environmentalism – in preference to joining or committing time to trade unions. As Frangi et al. (2020: 301) observe of the US:

> the locus of mobilisation has largely shifted from the workplace to society. Policy-focused advocacy campaigns beyond the workplace structured around a variety of organizations, identities (such as race, ethnicity, age and sexual orientation) and social justice issues are considered more effective in enhancing labour rights for low-wage, unrepresented and oppressed workers.

This may also be happening in the UK, another example of substitutes for traditional union action. Any such tendency may be accentuated by union amalgamations which have submerged small specialist unions into great conglomerates such as Unite and Unison whose purposely meaningless names no longer convey a distinct craft or occupational identity to form the basis of more traditional workplace solidarity.

A drift towards individualism and personal identity concerns, and away from collective solidarity, has probably been intensified by greater access to higher and further education and skills training. Better-qualified employees have a wider range of potential employers to choose from than was the case in the past. Rather than staying with one employer for long periods, as was more often the case when there were many nationalised industries and long-standing private sector employers, people with transfer-able skills and qualifications may now change jobs in pur-suit of higher pay, rather than relying on union-achieved pay increases. As the Resolution Foundation has shown (Cominetti et al. 2022), moving to a new employer offers a greater pay increase than staying in existing employment – with workers who leave to take up work in booming sec-tors doing best of all. Those in heavily unionised sectors, such as public administration, tend to change jobs less frequently and rely on collective bargaining to boost their pay. Those who are more mobile have less incentive to join a union.

The proportion of workers changing jobs has increased in all age groups, but the young are the most mobile, and this may be one reason why union membership has fallen most sharply among young people.

If we look at the youngest age groups, back in 1995 6.4% of employees aged 16–19 were in unions, but by 2022 this had fallen to 2.4%; the corresponding figures for 20–24-year-olds were 19.3% and 8.9% respectively. Mean-while, the unionisation rate for those aged 55–59 had only fallen from 38.6% to 30.9%, while that for 60–64-year-olds had barely shifted – from 30.2% to 29.2%. Unionised workers have always been on average rather older than other employees, but this is no longer just a life-stage effect. Unions are failing to recruit younger workers in sufficient numbers to replace those retiring. Unions are increasingly representing older workers, which may accentuate conservative tendencies and resistance to change in the workplace.

Another change from the past, implicit in the public–private distribution of union membership, is in educational qualifications. Whereas union members used to be relatively poorly educated on average, this is no longer the case. On the contrary, union members are more likely (54.3%) to have a degree or equivalent than non-union members (42.2%). They are much more likely (43.5% to 24.5%) to be in a professional occupation than non-unionists.

Union density is greater in particular industries than others – mainly those in the public sector, but there is also some concentration in parts of manufacturing and in the transport sector.

Unionisation is also stronger in Northern Ireland, Wales and Scotland than in England, and in regions such as the North East and the North West than London and the South East. This partly reflects the concentration of public sector jobs in particular areas. It also reflects the fact that, where employment has grown the fastest, union density has correspondingly fallen the fastest.

The point to emphasise is that unionisation is not spread at random across the workforce, but that unionised workers have rather different characteristics from those of non-unionists. This is of relevance when we come to consider the effects of unionism in chapter 6.

Conclusion

The union movement today is a very different entity than that of the late 1970s and early 1980s. It is a feminised movement, embracing large numbers of highly educated professional workers disproportionately employed in the public sector and often concentrated in large unions with little clear identity with particular trades, occupations or regional loyalties. The changes in British society and the British labour market which have brought this about are irreversible, and it is difficult at the moment to see a return to the high levels of unionisation achieved in the past.

Nevertheless, the union movement does cling to one tradition which goes back to its earliest years – reliance on the strike weapon, and the legal protections associated with it, in its pursuit of improved pay and conditions. I now turn to look at this.

5   STRIKES AND OTHER INDUSTRIAL ACTION

The strike weapon has been used for centuries. In modern conditions, a strike has been defined in the 1996 Employment Rights Act as 'a concerted refusal, or a refusal under a common understanding, of any number of employed persons to continue to work for an employer in consequence of a dispute'.

Other industrial action, or 'action short of a strike', can also be used to put pressure on an employer. This can, for example, cover overtime bans, or 'working to rule' – doing only what is specifically required by your contract.

Both strikes and other forms of industrial action must nowadays be agreed by an official ballot before they receive legal protection.[1] A ballot, which must be by post and supervised by a qualified scrutineer, can ask whether members approve of a strike, action short of a strike, or both: the latter option gives union officials some discretion over appropriate tactics. Without a ballot, any industrial action could render unions liable to damages. A vote for action is normally only valid for six months. After this period is up, another ballot has to be held in order for the action to continue.

---

1   Taking part in industrial action and strikes. UK Government (https://www .gov.uk/industrial-action-strikes).

The strike pattern

Figure 10 shows one measure of strike action in the post-war period: working days lost. The figures go up to the end of 2019; Covid disrupted union activity and data collection over the next two and a half years.

Figure 10 Thousands of working days lost to disputes 1950–2019 (year to December)

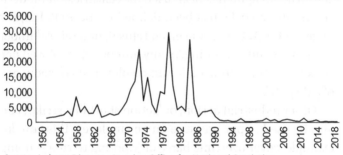

Source: Labour Disputes Inquiry, Office for National Statistics.

What is apparent from this chart is that strike activity over the thirty years from 1990 was far lower than in the 1960s, 1970s and 1980s. Working days lost peaked at almost 30 million in 1979 (in a much smaller workforce than today), with the 1984 miners' strike a close second. After 1990, days lost fluctuated around a low level. The recent spate of strikes may have shocked a generation which has never seen industrial action on such a scale. But to put it into perspective, in the year from June 2022 (when the recent round of strikes began to take off) to end-May 2023, the total number of working days lost was just short of 4 million, less than 15% of the 1979 total – and, incidentally, a tiny fraction of the 185 million days lost to sickness absence in 2022.[2]

Figure 11 Annual average days lost to strikes per 1,000 employees 2010–19

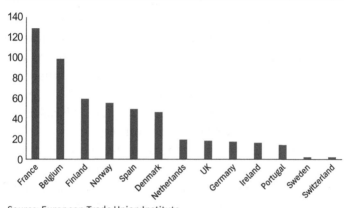

Source: European Trade Union Institute.

It's also worth bearing in mind that the UK's strike record in the decade before Covid was modest compared with other European countries such as France and Belgium (as Figure 11 illustrates). Even at the higher post-Covid rate the UK will not be an outlier internationally, as there has been a recent upsurge in strikes in France, Portugal,

---

2 While this is a comparison often trotted out, what to make of it? If 100,000 workers in a sector go on strike for a day, this is potentially very disruptive with much greater knock-on effects on the wider economy (as pointed out shortly) than is the case if 100,000 random people across the country take the day off with the sniffles. Yet the direct loss of output as conventionally measured appears to be the same.

Greece, Germany and the Netherlands as well as the UK,[3] possibly the result of pent-up issues during lockdown now bursting to the surface.

Taking a longer perspective, what are the ostensible reasons for strikes? The Office for National Statistics[4] notes that between 1999 and 2018, around 75% of all UK working days lost were in disputes over pay. Other reasons included staffing and work allocation, working conditions and supervision and redundancy; sometimes more than one issue was in play at the same time. Disputes which appear to be about a particular concern may also be reflecting other underlying problems or grievances.

There are, however, changes in the recorded causes and frequency of disputes as economic conditions change. Disputes over pay are more common in periods of rapid inflation – the 1970s winter of discontent being a case in point – while disputes over redundancies feature strongly in economic downturns. For example, the recession following the financial crisis meant rising job losses and unemployment: thus in 2009 60% of working days lost were over redundancies, rising to 86% of days lost in the following year.

As might be expected given the pattern of union membership, strikes are typically far more common in the public sector than in the private sector. Public sector

3   The EU labour strike map: the rise and fall of industrial action. *EU Observer*, 11 April 2023 (https://euobserver.com/health-and-society/156905).

4   https://www.ons.gov.uk/employmentandlabourmarket/peopleinwork/ workplacedisputesandworkingconditions/articles/theimpactofstrikesin theuk/june2022tofebruary2023#overview

employment between January 1996 and May 2023 averaged around 20% of employees, but the public sector accounted for 60% of all disputes, and 70% of all working days lost, in that period. The reclassification of groups of employees – some rail workers, Royal Mail, some college employees, even some bank employees following the financial crash – has moved them between sectors in the data. This may confuse matters, but the general picture is clear. Strike activity in the 2020s is primarily a public sector activity, or involves private sector businesses which were once in the public sector and retain high levels of unionisation.

In the past, private sector strikes were of greater importance. For example, although public sector workers may have enthusiastically joined the Winter of Discontent in 1978–79, that industrial relations disaster was set off by 72,000 Ford car workers going on unofficial strikes which led to them breaching the government's 5% pay target by winning a 17% pay increase. This was immediately followed by lorry drivers pushing for an even higher increase (Whitton 2016). Similar private sector action has not been a feature of recent strikes.

How do strikes play out?

The way in which economists analysed strikes in the last century is in a framework developed by Sir John Hicks (1963: ch. 7) in the 1930s. Assume a situation where a private sector employer and union are initially miles apart. The union makes a high wage demand, while the employer makes a paltry offer. A strike results. As the strike proceeds, both sides incur costs and adjust their position. In Figure 12 the 'union resistance curve' slopes downwards, flattening out at a very low wage rate where workers would leave the job; the 'employer concession curve' slopes upward, but reaches a maximum where paying a higher wage would bankrupt the firm. As the diagram indicates, there will be a wage rate at which these curves cross, and this is where a settlement can occur. Both parties would be worse off if the strike continued beyond t^*.

Figure 12 A 'classic' strike

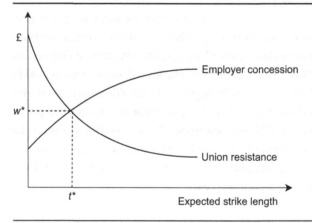

Hicks discusses the factors determining the position and shape of these curves, but also makes the important point that a strike could be avoided if each party knew with certainty the true costs faced by the other. Then they could proceed to the settlement at w^* without the need for a strike, with both parties better off.

Needless to say, the parties don't know each other's true position – indeed they both have an incentive to conceal it. So Hicks's argument suggests that anything which brings the parties together – extended negotiations, conciliation services and so on – helps to increase knowledge of the other side's position and will hasten a settlement. This became the orthodoxy in industrial relations thinking in the post-war period.

There's much to be said in favour of this way of thinking about strikes. An implication of Hicks's analysis is that the power of a union in winning higher pay is not necessarily connected to the number of strikes it 'wins', but by the strength of the threat the union poses to a business's profits. A successful union may strike rarely, because the business realises that it would be more damaged by a strike than by meeting the union's demands and the union itself knows how far to push. Hicks's approach was built on by Siebert and Addison (1981), who saw strikes being caused by disruption to bargaining expectations, with greater uncertainty ('accidents' such as unanticipated inflation) leading to more strikes.

It does suggest that strikes will end sooner rather than later, and that both parties are rational in a narrow sense of wanting to do the best they can. But it is a model of the behaviour of profit-seeking private sector employers who have to reach a settlement to stay in business, and unions (and their members) with few resources to fall back on.

Moreover, strikes are now no longer for the continuous extended period assumed by Hicks. Public sector unions, with significant strike funds and members who are normally better off than private sector workers, typically strike for a day or a few days at a time.[5] The costs to members are limited, and in some cases made up for in overtime later. Meanwhile, public sector employers are under little compulsion to reach a settlement. Their 'business' may be disrupted by strikes, but the civil service or schools or the passport service will not go bust: indeed they may save money. So strikes can drag on indefinitely.

Whereas private sector strikes are aimed at imposing costs on employers and their shareholders, public sector strikes are clearly undertaken to impose costs on the public: parents whose children can't go to school, NHS patients who have to wait for treatment, university students whose lectures are cancelled. The aim is to get the public so vexed that they turn on the government, which is then forced to settle.

A further complication is that public sector activists are often not in it just to increase pay. At the extreme, some may quite explicitly want to bring down the government.[6] More moderate unionists may demand more staff be employed (a rare demand in the private sector) or that policy

---

5   This is the case in other countries as well. In the US, 'traditional' strikes where employees withdraw labour for an indefinite period, are much less common than in the past. In 1970 there were 381 major strikes, but by 2014 there were only 11. Union action switched to intermittent or 'partial' strikes, despite this type of industrial action not being protected under the National Labor Relations Act (Landry 2016).

6   There is not a moment to waste – TUC must call general strike to bring down Tories and bring in a workers government! *The News Line*, 11 September 2023 (https://wrp.org.uk/editorials/there-is-not-a-moment-to-waste-tuc -must-call-general-strike-to-bring-down-tories-and-bring-in-a-workers -government/).

should change – for instance, that NHS services should not be contracted out, or that Ofsted scrap a round of school inspections. And, as we see on the railways, productivity bargains to boost pay – which sometimes work in the 'real' private sector, where trade-offs are more common and negotiators less absolutist – are anathema.

Public sector unions often do not seem to accept that there are limits to what employers can afford. Whereas in the private sector firms can and do go bust, and union members (or their officials) know that they cannot push too far, in the public sector there is no hard constraint. Unions know that if they get the public on their side, governments will often concede for the sake of a respite from the never-ending task of placating pressure from clamouring interest groups.

The cost of strikes

During periods of strike activity, there is often media discussion of the costs which strikes are imposing on 'the economy' or on the public. Both sides tend to exaggerate the costs strikes impose. Unions and their supporters want to emphasise how much employers and the public are losing out by not agreeing to their demands: critics point to the damage allegedly caused by irresponsible industrial action and urge strikers to go back to work.

Sorting out the real costs is a difficult question. There is only a limited and out-of-date academic literature on the topic – perhaps not surprising, given the reduced salience of the topic since the 1980s.

Economists tend to focus on the first-order economic effects of strikes in terms of reduced output. In principle, we measure this by the pay which workers lose plus the returns to other factors of production which are lost when work is stopped.

One of the few published estimates of the impact of the recent UK strikes on GDP, by the Centre for Economics and Business Research,[7] predicted direct costs totalling £1.2 billion for the year to June 2023. This was calculated by looking at those sectors where working days were lost to strike action, and multiplying days lost by average daily pay rates in these sectors plus a mark-up. These costs were summed to get an overall figure.

We could spend a lot of time quibbling over the details, but this looks about right. However, there would be offsets to this lost output. For if trains are not running, people will take more taxis, or may have to stay overnight in hotels. If junior doctors are on strike, consultants may be hired to take on their shifts (at exorbitant hourly rates[8]). GDP increases as a result, mitigating the direct output loss.

These offsets are only a part of the knock-on effects of strikes, though. If railway or tube staff are on strike, many of us can now work at home. Significant numbers cannot, however. They have to struggle into work, almost certainly

---

7   Industrial action cost the UK economy £243m in Q1 due to lost working days, but indirect costs will drive bigger overall impacts. Centre for Economics and Business Research, 12 May 2023 (https://cebr.com/reports/industrial-action-cost-the-uk-economy-243m-in-q1-due-to-lost-working-days-but-indirect-costs-will-drive-bigger-overall-impacts/).

8   £3k a shift – how doctor strikes cost NHS fortune. BBC News, 20 September 2023 (https://www.bbc.co.uk/news/health-66861960).

adding extra time to their commute and losing some working time. A back-of-the-envelope estimate: if 1 million people lost half an hour's work on 25 rail strike days in the year to end-May 2023, this would have meant a loss of GDP of at least £300 million. Others who cannot work at home, and cannot get in to work at all, lose a complete day's output. About 13% of those who normally travel to work by train, and are unable to work at home (questioned in July–October 2022), reported being unable to work at all during rail strikes (DfT 2023).

As a proportion of all workers, this would be small, perhaps less than 2%, but this could still mean a loss of output of £150 million or so per strike day. The total cost in lost output by non-rail workers prevented from working could then be of the order of £3.75 billion over the full year to June.

The rail strikes may also have damaged activities which depend on transport into our cities. Examples include retail, entertainment, hotels and restaurants around city centres, particularly in London. At the time of the June 2022 rail and underground strikes, the hospitality industry estimated that they would cost its members over half a billion pounds in lost business that week. In September 2023, the claim was now that the UK night-time hospitality business had lost £3.5 billion from strikes over the previous 15 months.[9] This sector has certainly had a hard time, both during lockdown and during transport strikes, but

---

9 Rail strikes cost hospitality £3.5bn. *The Spirits Business*, 25 September 2023 (https://www.thespiritsbusiness.com/2023/09/rail-strikes-cost-hospitality-3-5bn/).

these claims almost certainly exaggerate the effects on the economy as a whole.

There would definitely have been losses as a result of lower attendance at unrepeatable events such as sports fixtures and concerts. However, some spending would have been rearranged in time, with planned visits to London's hotels and theatres simply shifted to strike-free weeks which would then have experienced an increase over their expected revenue. There is some evidence that a similar sort of time-shifting effect occurs when there is an additional bank holiday (for instance, that for the late Queen's platinum jubilee) (DDCMS 2021).

There are other types of rearranged consumption which would offset some output losses. Retail spending may be diverted from city centres to out-of-town venues, or to on-line purchases. Similarly, suburban restaurants, bars and cinemas may have gained at the expense of the capital in strike weeks. Such shifts occur all the time for non-strike reasons, such as the weather.

So over the whole year, while the losses to some con-sumer-facing businesses in London and some other big cit-ies may indeed have been very significant, the overall net loss of output to the economy over the year was probably more modest, perhaps £1–2 billion.

Mention of geographical relocation of activity should remind us that strikes can vary considerably in impact around the country. For example, in London, well over half of all journeys to work take place via train, underground or bus, with only 28% by car. In Wales, just over 6% of travel to work is by bus or rail (no underground, of course), while

82% drive. Thus, a national rail strike has a big effect on London, but a far smaller effect elsewhere.

Some national strikes will have had a more equal impact around the country – the schools strikes, for example. Faced with the closure of schools, many parents will have had to take time off work. There are around 6.5 million working parents in the UK. According to an ONS (2023) survey, 31% of parents questioned said they would have to work fewer hours, and 28% reported that they would not be able to work at all.

This may be an exaggeration: when people are faced with an actual rather than a theoretical strike, they may find they can make arrangements with friends or relatives. But even if we assume just half of those who say they would have to stay at home actually do so, the cost in lost output from a day off work would total in excess of £240 million. Teachers have been on strike at varying times in the different UK nations, but if we assume an average of five days of school strikes during the year under consideration, the costs of parents' lost working time would be just over £1.2 billion.

One of the most problematic areas to assess knock-on effects is also one of the most controversial – the various disputes in the National Health Service. The ONS also examined the effects of the total of 16 days of strike action during December 2022 and January and February 2023. Output was certainly cut: apparently 'at least' 93,022 outpatient appointments, 18,716 elective procedures, 27,957 community service appointments and 9,634 mental health and learning disability appointments had to be rescheduled. These were the service losses correspond-ing to the loss of output measured by the value of days of strike action. But these delays in treatment will have im-plications for patients. Some may not have been able to re-turn to work as rapidly as they could have done, meaning further losses of output – and probably some premature deaths as well as the subjective costs of delay in terms of pain, distress and apprehension.

Delays might have been even greater if the NHS had not hired extra doctors and nurses to cover for striking staff. The NHS's Chief Financial Officer has said that the cost of April 2023's 5-day junior doctors' strike alone included £100 million spent on paying more senior staff at premium rates to cover for junior colleagues. Again, however, des-pite the costs to the NHS of these extra payments, they actually added to GDP, as noted earlier, partly offsetting the loss of output from the strikers.

There are other, less obvious knock-on costs. Strikes by Royal Mail and Civil Service unions will have caused delays in receiving important documents and dealing with legal permissions and obligations.

The conclusions to be drawn from this brief survey are, first, that the costs of strike action to the economy are slip-pery to define, as in some cases consumers switch spending in the face of strikes so that the loss to one organisation or business may be offset by a gain to another. Second, how-ever, that there are inevitably knock-on effects as strikes prevent individuals in other parts of the economy from working, or force them to incur extra costs. Third, it is clear that the total cost of strikes is a multiple of the direct costs in lost output from strikers. Fourth, that the cost of strikes in key areas such as transport, education and healthcare is borne largely by businesses which are not party to the disputes, and by the general public.

A rough estimate of the overall costs associated with the rash of strike activity beginning in the middle of 2022, and still going on at the time of writing in November 2023, would put the figure at £5 billion or so, a multiple of the direct loss of output in the striking businesses or organisations. This may be thought to be relatively low in the context of a total GDP of £2.2 trillion in 2022, though note that it does not take account of longer-term effects of regular strike action in terms of discouraging investment, or deterring management from pushing necessary productivity-enhancing changes to work organisation, thus reducing growth in the longer term.

Bear in mind too that, with most of the recent strikes being in the public or quasi-public sector where consumers face little choice, the effectiveness of strike action from the union perspective is not gauged by damage to the profitability of shareholders in capitalist firms, but by whether the strike will sufficiently hurt the ordinary citizen to such an extent that the government will acquiesce to union demands. This, rather than the exact cost in lost GDP, is perhaps the real issue which should be debated.

Other industrial action

In addition to strike action, unions can engage in 'action short of a strike' (ASOS). This covers any action which imposes pressure on the employer, but which does not amount to a full withdrawal of labour. It normally involves little cost to the employee, but can impose a significant cost on the employer and hence to the customer or the general public. It accordingly requires a ballot in order to protect the union and unionists from possible legal action.

ASOS can cover a variety of generic areas, such as 'working to rule' (where employees perform their duties strictly in the terms of their contract and refuse to do anything else); 'go slow' (which involves deliberately working at a slower pace); a 'sit in' or a 'work in' (where employees under threat of dismissal occupy the employer's premises); or overtime bans.

In practical terms, action short of a strike can often achieve as much as, maybe more than, a full-on strike. For example, the train drivers' union ASLEF has frequently banned overtime and non-rostered working; this has led to many cancellations of train services. It has also banned cover for missing drivers, and stopped existing drivers assisting in training new ones, thus extending a shortage of drivers and delaying the introduction of new trains. In universities, we have recently seen a union boycott of examinations and a refusal to mark exam scripts. This led to many unfortunate students having to 'graduate' without having formal results available, a good example of how union action can severely penalise people who are not directly involved in a dispute. In this case, ASOS has created far more damage than the rather ineffectual series of one-day strikes which the lecturers' union, UCU, has held. And, unlike strikes, this type of action often in practice may not lead to a loss of pay to those involved, given the complexities of calculating individual responsibilities.

Other tactics

Unions may also have other ways of pursuing objectives. One is a consequence of the increasing regulation of the labour market and the growth in importance of employment tribunals. Although, as suggested earlier, this may have worked against unions' traditional role in the workplace, it is also the case that unions have been able to use the tribunal system, and the law generally, to push their agenda.

Unions will often support individuals in their tribunal claims,[10] but they have to be selective given their limited resources. However, in some cases they may help organise what amount to 'class actions', where a number of claimants put in similar claims with union support in the hope of achieving a new interpretation of labour law which will advance union objectives.

For example, the GMB union helped Uber drivers win a series of tribunal claims to be recognised as 'workers' rather than independent contractors. This entitled up to 30,000 drivers to guaranteed minimum wages, holiday pay and breaks, and many to significant compensation.[11] Similarly,

---

10 For example, securing holiday pay to which an employee is entitled (https://www.thompsonstradeunion.law/news/news-releases/employment-matters/key-victory-for-unison-at-tribunal-voluntary-overtime-counts-towards-holiday-pay).

11 Uber drivers entitled to workers' rights after Supreme Court ruling. *Leighday*, 21 February 2021 (https://www.leighday.co.uk/news/news/2021-news/uber-drivers-entitled-to-workers-rights-after-supreme-court-ruling/).

GMB has backed a long-running equal pay case against the supermarket chain Asda. Predominantly female store staff claim that they should be paid the same as the mainly male staff working in depots. Should the case ultimately succeed, it will have implications for all other supermarkets and could ultimately substantially boost retail staff's pay and cost the industry many billions of pounds.[12]

Results like these achieve far more than unions could hope to gain through conventional collective bargaining, and illustrate how far the industrial relations environment has moved from the voluntarist orientation of the 1960s. Today, the labour market is highly regulated, and unions have learnt how to use this to the advantage of their membership.

We may take issue with the extent of employment regulation, but support of tribunal claims is a valid role for unions. So are some of the social media campaigns run by unions to put pressure on employers. More controversial are the techniques employed under the heading of 'leverage', a tactic particularly associated in Britain with Unite the Union.[13]

Leverage involves unconventional ways of putting pressure on a business, perhaps involving the company's directors (and sometimes even their families), shareholders, investors, customers and suppliers. A union may try to create difficulty for an employer by organising or facilitating

---

12 Asda workers win key appeal in equal pay fight. BBC News, 26 March 2021 (https://www.bbc.co.uk/news/business-56534988).

13 Leverage campaigns and how they work. Wales Institute of Social and Economic Research and Data, 30 September 2021 (https://wiserd.ac.uk/blog/leverage-campaigns-and-how-they-work/).

media stories, using sympathetic Parliamentary commit-tees[14] and social media campaigns both directly against the firm and against its suppliers and clients. It may or-ganise demonstrations or questions at company AGMs. It may involve picketing at different locations; in one notori-ous case Unite arranged for thirty people to stand outside the home of one director, and sent 'wanted' posters to the daughter of another.

Such measures can be effective, though they could tip over into intimidation. They may also be intended to mis-lead as to the real degree of support for a campaign, and may need to be monitored.

Conclusion

Strike action today is mainly concentrated in the public sector, and it is at levels which, though higher than for many years, remain far below those of the 1970s and 1980s. Today's strikes typically take the form of an intermittent series of one- or two-day strikes, rather than an extended period of withdrawal of labour of the kind we saw, for example, in the miners' strike of 1984–85. Strikes in the public sector or quasi-public sector are consciously aimed at inconveniencing the public, with the intention that this will then lead the government to agree to union demands in order to appease voters. The cost of strikes, though

---

14 An example is the way in which the House of Commons Business, Innova-tion and Skills Committee took up Unite's campaign against Sports Direct (https://publications.parliament.uk/pa/cm201617/cmselect/cmbis/219/219.pdf).

modest in relation to the economy as a whole, hits some sectors hard and totals considerably more than the direct costs in terms of the lost output of strikers.

Most strikes are over pay, particularly when prices are rising rapidly, but sometimes about other working conditions such as hours and rest periods. However, in economic downturns, job losses and redundancies become more important. For some activists, the objective goes beyond traditional focus on pay and conditions to demand changes in government policy – and even, in some cases, changes in the government.

Strikes attract much attention in the media, but are only one weapon in unions' armoury. Various forms of action short of a strike can often have a considerable impact. Unions have had some success with group claims through employment tribunals, and also with unorthodox ways of pressuring businesses to accede to their demands.

How far strikes succeed in meeting their objectives is a moot point. The recent round of strikes has seen relatively few unions achieve pay increases in excess of inflation, although there are still some major disputes, for example, on the railways and for NHS doctors, where the outcome remains uncertain at the time of writing. It may be that other tactics now have more success than this centuries-old manifestation of union strength.

However, the outcome of particular strikes or other industrial action is probably less important for unions and the economy in the long run than the effects of union activity over time. It is this topic which the next chapter explores.

6 THE ECONOMIC EFFECTS OF UNIONS

There is a considerable academic literature, of varying degrees of sophistication, on the longer-run economic effects of trade unionism. This covers the effects on the level of wages, the dispersion of wages, working conditions, health and safety, productivity, and a number of other issues.

The relative wage effect

Wages are certainly the most researched area. Some early economists – Adam Smith, for example – seem to have thought that unions could raise pay. Others, however – Ricardo and Malthus among them – demurred, believing that in the long run competition in product markets would eliminate firms which paid in excess of the 'natural' level of wages. Their view was echoed in modern times by Milton Friedman and other Chicago economists. Others, however, have taken the view that firms with continuing product market power generate 'rents' which unions can grab a share of over long periods.

There are a number of reasons why we might expect trade union members to be paid more than non-members (Bryson 2007, 2014). The most obvious is that unions force pay up through collective bargaining. Another related reason might be that they are better able to resist cuts in wages during economic downturns (leading to the prediction that the 'trade union premium' or the 'relative wage effect'[1] tends to increase during recessions as non-unionists face pay cuts).

A more subtle reason why there might be a union premium emphasises that a union, by forcing up wages, may reduce employment. This means that some workers cannot get jobs in unionised businesses, and are thus forced into the non-unionised sector, where the increased supply forces down wages. However, this means that the size of the trade union premium exaggerates the gain to workers from union membership. It also suggests a loss to the economy as a result of moving workers from more productive to less productive jobs.

More positively, a union premium could persist because union members are less likely to change jobs; over time this makes them more experienced, and encourages employers to invest in training. Their enhanced 'firm-specific human capital' (Bryson 2014: 3) thus makes them more productive, justifying paying them more than non-union 'outsiders'. Furthermore, as higher-paying union jobs are in short supply, employers have a queue of applicants from which to choose the best workers. Again, the average productivity of unionised employees rises, making higher pay compatible with profitability.

---

1 The percentage relative wage effect is $[(W_u - W_n)/W_n] \times 100$, where W_u is the union wage and W_n the non-union wage.

However, things may not work out like this. There may be a 'threat effect' (Rosen 1969) of unionism which raises the relative pay of non-union members. In this view, employers who do not want the potentially disruptive influence of unions may be willing to pay workers extra to obviate the threat. This tactic may not be explicit: workers in firms which pay well may just see less need to join a union. Where the tactic succeeds, the union membership premium may be non-existent.

Another factor tending to minimise the membership premium is the coverage of collective bargaining. As we have seen, where unions are recognised, bargaining covers both union and non-union members. So in the public sector, 88% of all workers were covered by collective bargaining in 2022, although union membership was only 48.6%. In the private sector the figures were 32.6% and 13% respectively. As explained in chapter 1, the non-unionists get a 'free ride' on union bargaining: they get any pay increase negotiated by unions without contributing to the cost of organisation and negotiation.

This all means that a simple comparison of union and non-union members, such as that shown in Figure 13, can tell us rather little about the effect of union membership on hourly earnings. It certainly cannot tell us what earnings would have been in the absence of unions, a comparison with which would give us the 'true' effect of unions. The direction of the trend in this figure may, however, be indicative. The sharp decline in the 'raw' premium in the last few years probably reflects the relative decline in pay in the (heavily unionised) public sector, which has fuelled the recent increase in industrial action.

Figure 13 Trade union wage premium (%) 1995–2022

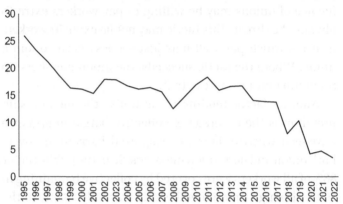

Note: Unadjusted wage premium of trade union members over non-union members (hourly earnings).
Source: BEIS.

However, as we saw in chapter 4, union members are not representative of the workforce as a whole. They are typically older, more experienced, hold higher qualifications, and so on. This means that, even in the absence of union membership, they would tend to earn more than the average worker because they possess characteristics which are valued by employers. This means that serious analysis of the effects of unions on pay have to model what union members would have been paid if they were not unionised in order to estimate the 'adjusted' premium (Bryson 2014).

There have been many attempts to do this with different data sets and different model specifications. Typically,

THE ECONOMIC EFFECTS OF UNIONS

the 'adjusted' premium is significantly less than the 'raw' premium and in some cases appears to be zero or even negative, although the effect for poorly paid workers (including some minority ethnic groups) appears to be greater than for better-paid workers and for women than for men (Bryson et al. 2019). There also seems to be a big difference in the union premium between the public and private sectors, something worth flagging up. Blanch-flower and Bryson (2010) find that, after controlling for workplace characteristics, worker occupations, qualifications, job characteristics and demographic factors, the public sector union premium in 2004 was about twice that in the private sector.

Unions and inequality

An implication of the existence of a membership premium would seem to be that unions tend to increase inequality within the labour market, representing an elite group of older, more educated, more skilled workers which is able to secure higher earnings.

This is an interpretation of the labour market which is rejected by union supporters. They point out that unions have historically insisted on workers in the same or similar jobs being paid the same. They have, for example, resisted performance-related pay, which they argue to be open to favouritism and could undermine pay settlements for the collectivity. Thus one thing about which there is reasonable consensus in the research literature is that, even if unions might act to increase inequality across the economy, they tend to reduce the dispersion of pay within unionised organisations. Evidence from the US and Canada (Card et al. 2018) suggests that the effect is much stronger in the public sector than in the private sector, and it is reasonable to assume that this is true in the UK as well.

There might be a case for saying that this may make labour markets more competitive, as pay variations are clearer and more obvious and that this could assist labour mobility and job matching. However, it is also true that unions could make labour markets work less efficiently, if rewards for individual effort are suppressed by union egalitarianism and if rigid wage structures lead to short-ages of some types of workers and excess supplies of others. Some problems of public sector pay might be associated with the narrowness of differentials.

One issue which concerns many labour market ana-lysts is possible discrimination against minority ethnic groups and women. Unions nowadays are very vocal in their opposition to discrimination. They have cleaned up an act which was sometimes distinctly grubby in the past. W. H. Hutt (1954), who had a strong influence on Hayek's concerns about unions, pointed to white trade unions as a major force behind South Africa's apartheid system – and in Britain there was something rather simi-lar in various places. Railway unions kept women and mi-nority workers out of the better-paid jobs for many years (Wolmar 2022: 194–97), while the TGWU's colour bar on Bristol buses in the 1950s and 1960s is notorious. More-over, though the London dockers' 1968 march in support of Enoch Powell[2] is often remembered, it is forgotten that this support was also manifested in more than 20 strikes, involving 10–12 thousand workers across the country. This involved, for example, brewery workers in Wolverhampton, motor panel workers in Coventry and power station workers in Staffordshire (Baroda 2021). And as late as 1969, the TUC General Council resisted rank and file calls for positive action to combat discrimination (Sullivan n.d.).

Nowadays, however, there seems to be a smaller pay gap between white and minority workers where unions are present (Forth et al. 2023). Relatedly, it appears that the rather more frequently discussed gender pay gap may be smaller in workplaces where unions are present (Elvira and Saporta 2001). However, this is complicated because, in settings where women form the majority, such as in some public sector occupations, unions may downplay wages and foreground other objectives such as job flexibility. A trade-off may be involved.

Other union 'premia'

This draws attention to the important point made by Freeman (1981), Freeman and Medoff (1984: ch. 4) and Buchmueller et al. (2004): unions may not just pursue higher earnings, but other objectives as well. In the US context, Freeman and Medoff (1984: 61) mention 'pensions,

---

2   In April 1968, Enoch Powell was sacked from the Conservative Shadow Cabinet by Edward Heath for making a provocative speech about immigration.

life insurance, major medical benefits, dental insurance, prepaid legal assistance, paid vacation, and payments for holidays' as fringe benefits which unions may help workers secure. At the time, they claimed, over half of labour costs in large firms went on benefits of this kind.

To the extent that this is significant, there would be other union premia in addition to the wage premium. Given the existence of a welfare state and more extended labour market regulation, benefits of this kind may not have been as significant in this country, but they still exist. There has only been limited research on this issue in the UK, and what there has been is rather out of date. However, reviewing the influence of trade unions in a paper for the TUC, Bryson and Forth (2017: 6) conclude that the literature shows that 'workplaces with recognised unions are more likely to provide extra-statutory sick pay, employer-provided pensions, special paid leave for emergencies, and subsidised childcare'. In their own research, Forth and Bryson (2019) find a substantial union premium on paid holidays, larger than the relative wage effect. The premium has, however, fallen as legislation has increased holiday entitlements for all – an example of the point made in chapter 4, that state provision now provides a substitute for some of the benefits which unions have historically provided. This is likely to be true also of the other benefits referred to in the TUC report: since the early 2000s, we have seen increases in state-mandated leave arrangements, auto-enrolment in pension schemes, and childcare subsidies.

Freeman and Medoff (1984) argue that, by providing union workers with a voice, they are able to convey to management that employees might prefer a different combination of wages and other benefits that businesses, ignorant of worker preferences, would otherwise provide. Thus they might provide a Pareto-optimal gain if firms can cut back on pay offers but increase some other benefits on a cost-neutral basis.

An obvious implication of this is that a concentration on the union wage premium can understate both the real gain to workers and the real cost to employers. A further implication is that changes in the measured wage premium might reflect not a decline in union bargaining strength, but rather a shift of preferences over time as wages become relatively less important, and at the margin, a new generation of workers value more highly shorter hours, working from home, or other flexible employment options.

Unions and job satisfaction

This leads on to another question which has concerned many commentators. If unions bring benefits to their members in terms of pay and other goodies, does it not follow that they will be more satisfied with their jobs, and enjoy greater well-being than non-members? You might think so, but for a long time, economists have doubted this. Early empirical work by Borjas (1979: 38) found that 'on average, union members report significantly *lower* levels of job satisfaction' than non-union members, with this result holding 'within occupational categories and across types of union'. Other studies supported this finding; a few years later Freeman and Medoff (1984: 196) wrote:

> In survey after survey of job satisfaction ... union workers
> ... report themselves less satisfied with most facets of their
> work, notably overall job satisfaction and supervisory
> treatment.

Economists have offered two possible explanations, cate-
gorised as the 'voice' and 'sorting' hypotheses. As we have
seen, Freeman and Medoff emphasised voice in their work,
taking the line that unions offer a way to articulate critical
attitudes towards the workplace. In order to build support,
unions have to draw attention to the downsides of workers'
jobs. An alternative view is that workers who experience
poor working conditions, or are perhaps naturally discon-
tented with their lot, will be more likely to join a union.
Workers either 'sort' into union membership or stay outside. In this view (Laroche 2017):

> it's not that being unionized makes employees less sat-
> isfied; it's that being the type of person who's often dis-
> satisfied or working in a place where there's lots to be
> dissatisfied about makes you more likely to join a union.

Work by Laroche (2016) and by Bessa et al. (2020) tends
to support this view, with union membership not being a
causative factor in correlations between membership and
job satisfaction or other well-being indicators.

Other research in this area has pointed out that the bulk
of the studies finding a negative union–job satisfaction relationship have been conducted in the US or the UK. But
perhaps this relationship may not exist in other industrial

relations contexts. Thus Hipp and Rolins Gavan (2015), in a cross-national study, find that the relationship between union membership and job satisfaction is contingent on the industrial relations system in particular countries, with factors such as union density, bargaining coverage and centralisation or decentralisation of bargaining playing an important part.

In a similar vein, van der Meer, using European Social Survey data, argues that the negative union effect does not exist for continental Western Europe. He puts this down to the centralisation of collective bargaining in much of the continent, which tends to remove conflict from the immediate workplace, and through the 'empowerment' of workers in social partner regimes. By empowerment, van der Meer (2019: 307) says:

> I mean that employees gain decision rights, or influence, over how the organization is managed, which goes beyond autonomy in their own jobs.

If the union–job satisfaction relationship varies geographically, it may also vary over time. In a wide-ranging article which appears to overturn more than 40 years of assumptions, Blanchflower et al. (2022) draw on analysis of surveys covering 2 million respondents from Europe and the US. Far from union membership being associated with discontent, these authors now find 'partial correlation between union membership and employee job satisfaction is positive and statistically significant' (p. 255). What appears to have happened around the turn of the century, they claim, is a switch in the UK and the US from a negative relationship to a positive one. This may have resulted from the changing institutional and legal environment, it may partly reflect business cycle fluctuations which make union members appreciate their relatively privileged position in economic downturns, or it may be a cohort (generational) effect.

On this latter point, a possibility is that 'changes in the industrial and occupational composition of unionized workers' (p. 275) may account for a flip in attitudes. A growing proportion of the shrunken union movement in both the US and Europe is made up of white collar or professional workers in the public sector, who may very well have different attitudes from those of the blue-collar workers who used to dominate union membership. They may be treated differently in their day-to-day work and have much less fear of losing their jobs in recessions.

So the result of this, if Blanchflower and colleagues are to be believed, is that union membership does now after all tend to be associated with greater job satisfaction, though quite why this is, and how permanent it is, remains unclear.

Union effects on productivity

If wage effects, other union premia and job satisfaction are measures of benefits to union members, economists have often been more concerned with wider effects on the economy. We have already noted that union benefits may be at the expense of costs to others – for instance, workers being displaced into non-union employment if unions reduce employment in unionised firms and sectors, or businesses and individuals impacted by lengthy strike action.

There is also a considerable literature on the effects of unions on productivity. Of course, there is a trivial sense in which unions forcing up wages for members necessarily increases the marginal revenue productivity of those continuing in employment, but this is achieved by forcing up prices where possible, and by cutting employment.

More importantly, there is an effect on overall productivity in the economy if union action diverts workers from high-productivity to low-productivity jobs, or creates or lengthens the duration of unemployment. On the point of duration of unemployment, for example, the employment protection literature (Scarpetta 2014) suggests that restrictions on firing workers (such as might be reinforced by powerful unions) slow exits into unemployment – but also delay rehiring, as businesses become reluctant to take on employees in uncertain recoveries. The longer people remain unemployed, the greater the loss of output and the more likely it is that skills and morale will deteriorate.

To the extent that unions distort labour market outcomes and lead to inefficient allocation of human and physical resources, there is a deadweight loss to the economy (Hirsch 1997: 5). However, the bulk of research on union effects on productivity avoids this broad macroeconomic perspective and is concerned with the impact of unionisation on particular firms and industries.

There are many ways in which unions can affect labour productivity (Barth et al. 2020a). On the negative side, union-imposed pay structures may distort incentives and efforts; restrictive practices such as over-staffing and resistance to innovative technology may hold back productivity directly; constant disputes and time-consuming grievances may displace management time and focus; job protection and rigid contracts may prevent necessary adjustment to economic change. There may also be problems if union-enforced job security reduces management's ability to impose necessary work discipline, with excessive unauthorised absences[3] and shirking.

On the other hand, if union action boosts pay but reduces employment, as in the right-to-manage framework, there will be a queue for jobs in unionised firms. This will enable management to be choosy and pick more able and committed workers. These workers will be more likely, because of the higher pay, to stay with the firm. This will reduce turnover and recruitment costs, and encourage employer investment in training and capital equipment, which will in turn boost productivity.

However, some of these 'positive' effects on productivity may, like relative wage effects, be at the expense of other participants in the economy. A less ambiguous source of gains was that first analysed by Freeman and Medoff (1984), mentioned earlier. In this view, unions give 'voice' to the preferences and knowledge of employees, thus enabling

---

3 Veliziotis (2010), using UK Labour Force Survey data for 2006–8, finds that 'trade union membership is associated with a substantial increase in the probability of reporting sick and in the amount of average absence taken.' This result can be largely attributed, he claims, to the protection that unions offer to unionised employees.

employers to have a clearer understanding of their workforce and assisting in joint problem-solving.

It is likely that in any workplace both these sets of effects are working. Research studies have therefore inevitably concentrated on the net effect of forces operating in both directions.

In the last thirty to forty years, there have been dozens, perhaps hundreds, of empirical studies of the effects of unions on productivity. These differ in the data sources (which may be cross-sectional, longitudinal or panel), the level (firm or industry) studied, and the model specifications (which differ in mathematical form and in the 'moderating' variables – such as closed-shop arrangements, union recognition, multi-unionism – which qualify the effects of unionisation on productivity). Although some apparent constancies can be found in simple qualitative comparisons of different studies – such as the net effect being relatively modest (Addison 2020: 5) – a more rigorous assessment comes from meta-analyses (Doucouliagos and Laroche 2003; Doucouliagos et al. 2017).

A meta-analysis in this context is used to evaluate empirical research by quantification of the factors causing differences in union effects on productivity between studies.[4]

---

4   The approach (Doucouliagos et al. 2017: 35)

   offers a scientific basis for reviewing the evidence base of union effects or other claimed relations between variables. It involves: a search for comparable studies, the coding of estimates and research dimensions, calculation of meta-averages, detection and correction for publication bias, and analysis of heterogeneity.

In their earlier study, Doucouliagos and Laroche (2003) found that, after controlling for differences between studies, there was a negative association between unions and productivity in the UK, but a positive association for the US. In the later work (Doucouliagos et al. 2017: 37):

> [W]e conclude that the impact on productivity varies by country and industry. For manufacturing, we find no effect for the United States, confirm the finding of an adverse effect for the United Kingdom, and find a positive effect for developing countries. In the case of other industries, we find positive productivity effects for construction, mining, and education. Taken together, the different industry and country effects yield a zero productivity effect overall.

Although these authors offer a magisterial view of the empirical literature, the issue can certainly never be regarded as closed. Recent work by Veliziotis and Vernon (2023), for example, suggests that in the UK things have changed since the millennium, with unionisation now being associated with higher productivity. The Thatcherite revolution is said to have broken the old union model in the UK's private sector, with restrictive practices scrapped and improved industrial relations in those firms where unions retain a strong presence. In these authors' view, the 'voice' effects of unionism are now to the fore.

But despite its recent publication, their study draws on data from the Workplace Employment Relations Survey from well over a decade ago, and it remains to be seen whether this improvement in productivity performance, if improvement there was, has been sustained. Certainly, looking at recent prominent industrial disputes, such as those on the railways[5] where over-staffing and the maintenance of restrictive practices continue to be a very visible feature of union policy, this may seem like wishful thinking.

Unions and employment growth

The consensus probably remains that unions have net negative effects on productivity in the UK. But even if the effects were to be minimally positive, it seems unlikely that they offset the increase in employment costs associated with union wage and other premia. The implication is then that profits are eroded, and also that share prices will be negatively affected. Both of these outcomes may deter investment and thus be associated over time with lower employment growth (Hirsch 1997: 5; Addison 2020: 6). Although, as always, there will be studies where this is shown not to be the case, Laroche (2020: 19), summarising findings from the US and the UK, states that 'the evidence points to a direct negative relationship between unionization and profitability'.

Even if firms in protected markets are able to maintain profits by passing costs on to consumers, this will likely lead to a fall in consumption and a consequent fall in employment below what it would otherwise have been.

---

5   The unions have, for example, opposed attempts to reorganise rosters to allow regular weekend working, one-person operation on trains, and changes to ticket offices.

This in turn may be one of the reasons why union density has declined in the private sector. If employment growth in unionised businesses is slower than in non-unionised businesses, and few new businesses become unionised, the overall unionisation rate will fall.

There is pretty strong evidence that unionised businesses are associated with slower employment growth. Indeed, this has been called 'the one constant' in empirical research about unions which, as always, contains a lot of 'on the one hand ... on the other'. Most studies have suggested that unions slow employment growth by 2–4 percentage points a year. Examples include for the US, Leonard (1992); for the UK, Blanchflower et al. (1991), Bryson (2004), Addison and Belfield (2004); for Canada, Walsworth (2010); for Australia, Wooden and Hawke (2000); and for Germany, Brändle and Goerke (2015).

Comment

It is clear that unions do have a measurable impact on a number of important economic variables. Despite the need to adjust a 'raw' premium to account for characteristics of union workers and their workplaces, there appear to be wage (and non-wage) benefits to union membership. However, these benefits appear to vary from group to group, and they may be stronger in the public sector than the private sector. The wage premium has probably declined, although it may be that union strength is now manifested in non-wage improvements such as reduced hours and flexible working.

Where do these benefits come from? Not in the main from productivity improvements, although as we have seen some researchers (Veliziotis and Vernon 2023) claim that in the UK unions may now have a positive effect on productivity. Even if they do still have a negative impact, among the research community there is an underlying sympathy for unions, as in this observation (Laroche 2020: 24):

> In a time of high and rising inequality, union activities almost invariably trade off some economic efficiency for greater justice in the workplace and reduced inequalities. This means that the existing studies that provide the evidence basis for ... [this report] ... are only one part of a decision system. They must also be evaluated relative to workers' and employers' social preferences and utility functions.

This seems to suggest that the costs of economic inefficiencies and welfare losses should be downplayed in favour of assertions about the benefits which union members obtain. But this is a political rather than an economic judgment.

Moreover, such costs are not merely abstract; they fall on other workers who are displaced into poorer-paying jobs (or none), consumers who pay higher prices, shareholders who get poorer returns, and – particularly given unions' strength in the public sector – taxpayers who pay more for public services. While union sympathisers may disagree, higher pay for unionised workers does not automatically serve to improve social justice.

7 TRADE UNIONS AND THE FUTURE

The story thus far: trade unions in Britain have a long history, leaving a pattern of industrial relations differing from that in other countries, with the state taking only a limited part in regulating negotiations over pay and conditions and the institutions involved. Although unions have modernised in many ways, after two hundred years they retain a distinct residue of the way in which they grew up. Part of this is a continuing element of suspicion, even antagonism, towards employers and governments – and an often uninhibited pursuit of sectional interest. Many employers in turn are still wary of unions, and in the newer private sector industries unions often play a negligible role. Their remaining muscle is in the public sector and some legacy private sector businesses which were for a long time in the public sector, such as Royal Mail, the utilities and the railways. The decline in overall union membership and union density over recent decades has many causes: it is common to most developed countries and should not be seen simply as the result of the Thatcher–Major industrial relations reforms.

I have observed that theoretical economic analysis of unions has never been particularly fruitful, replete as it is with classic two-handed conclusions. On the one hand, unions can be seen as monopolists, using market power to secure higher wages and distort the allocation of labour. On the other, they can be seen as rebalancing the scales against employers who may themselves possess market power as monopsonists, forcing down wages below those which would prevail in a competitive market.

Differences of opinion may now be played out in a more formal analytical style, but this is essentially the same dispute as that which exercised economists two centuries ago. A more recent addition to the discussion came with Freeman and Medoff's argument that unions could offer 'voice' in the workplace and thus reduce labour dissatisfaction and turnover, allowing employers to offer a more appealing combination of pay and other conditions, and thus indirectly improving productivity – an argument which is attractive to the ever-growing number of HR professionals. But against this, counter-arguments stress that unions can also damage productivity through reducing organisations' ability to respond flexibly to change.

The last forty years have seen a proliferation of attempts to test propositions about unions, involving the application of steadily more sophisticated econometrics to more widely available datasets. This has clarified some issues, though by no means all. Summarising findings, it appears that union membership tends to boost pay, working conditions and fringe benefits, but by less than is often thought and at a declining rate over time as labour market legislation has usurped part of unions' role as workers' champions. It also appears that unions reduce inequality within workplaces.

The evidence on productivity is less clear, with much depending on context, but as we have seen, meta-analysis of empirical work tentatively suggests that overall in Britain unions have a negative effect. It does seem that profitability is lower in unionised workplaces, and one result which seems to be firmly established in studies from many different countries is that unionised businesses grow more slowly than non-unionised businesses.

The evidence that unions have an impact and produce benefits for their members does not enable us to say that unions serve some wider concept of economic or social justice. If unions reduce employment in better-paid sectors, for example, this may have the effect of crowding more workers into less-well-paid sectors and pushing pay there even lower. And though they may reduce inequality within unionised workplaces, they probably increase inequality between employees in different workplaces.

Will there be a union revival?

It may be that the recent round of strike activity will encourage a recovery in unionisation, but there have so far been few signs of this.[1] As suggested in chapter 4, the changes in our economy and society which have occurred

---

1 Though there has been an attempt by the GMB to unionise the Amazon warehouse in Coventry, seeking to emulate similar action in the US. Some have claimed that this is a straw in the wind. Amazon does not recognise the union and has taken steps to thwart recognition, but as many as 1,000 workers have been on strike in a continuing dispute (https://www.gmb.org.uk/news/coventry-amazon-workers-vote-to-extend-strike-for-six-months).

since the heyday of unionism in the 1970s and 1980s are not going to be reversed.

Some writers (Frangi et al. 2019) see unions as 'dinosaurs' which have failed to adapt to changes in society and in the ubiquity of social media. While unions may use Facebook, X and all the rest, they may have tended to do so as a form of 'broadcast' to spread the word, rather than engaging in the constant tweeting and retweeting which build supportive networks as well as union membership. These networks could act to pressure employers and government, amplifying union influence.

In this view, unions might also want to reorient towards campaigns to improve the lot of workers who are not currently unionised, and indeed could not easily be involved in traditional collective bargaining – freelance and even self-employed workers, for example.

The strikes which we have seen recently, however, reprise twentieth-century, even nineteenth-century, disputes where you can have set-piece confrontations with a large employer (nowadays very often the state or its functionaries) with a continuing existence. This is familiar, almost comforting, territory for the union movement. But unions have had relatively little to say about the emerging twenty-first-century environment of the 'gig' economy, where pop-up businesses appear and disappear overnight, there is increasing self-employment and contracting-out, contracts are only temporary and innovation and change are daily realities.

Some workers may thrive in this environment. Others may be vulnerable – but unions can't turn the clock back

and impose long-term, secure employment on companies which may not be here in two or three years' time
and whose business model requires greater employment
flexibility than unions are prepared to tolerate. Workers
in today's more fluid world arguably benefit from unions
which rediscover their 'friendly society', self-help roots
– offering insurance, freestanding pensions, help with
mortgages, legal advice, assistance with job search and so
on. This may be where any future growth of unionism lies,
rather than in old-style confrontation with large employers and government, which comprise only a part of today's
mind-bogglingly diverse labour markets.

Old-time religion

But if unions cannot easily reinvent themselves, it is
tempting for their officials to ask if government action
can artificially revive old-fashioned unionisation to some
degree. Should the government attempt to do so? Many on
the Left would argue it could and it should. For example,
the IPPR (Institute for Public Policy Research) Economic
Justice Commission, a grouping of the Great and Good
from the Archbishop of Canterbury downwards, made a
detailed case for such intervention in a widely publicised
report (IPPR 2018). This seems to have made a considerable impression on the Labour Party leadership, which
plans to implement many of its suggestions now it is back
in government.

The IPPR claimed that unions are a necessary element
in securing economic justice, though little attempt was

made to justify this assertion or review the arguments against. The report argued for a doubling of collective bargaining coverage to 50% of workers by 2030. Specific proposals to achieve this included a new 'right to access' that would require organisations to allow unions physical access to workplaces to talk to workers and recruit members. This should be combined with a 'digital right of access' to reach remote workers and a new 'right to join' spelt out formally in workers' contracts. The Commission also proposed a trial of auto-enrolment into trade unions within the 'gig' economy, on the model of auto-enrolment into workplace pensions, and a WorkerTech Innovation Fund to support unions to innovate and use digital technology to recruit and organise.

A paper written for the Commission went into more detail of these and other proposals. One example (Dromey 2018: 26):

> In order to reverse the decline in collective bargaining and to boost pay and productivity, the government should seek to promote sectoral collective bargaining in key sectors.

This proposal has frequently been made. It is likely to be easier and cheaper for unions to negotiate for whole sectors than to deal with separate employers. The decline in such sector-wide bargaining has already been noted.

The case for reviving it has sometimes been linked to a well-known academic paper by Lars Calmfors and John Driffill (1988). Writing at a time of generally high unemployment in Europe, they argued that macroeconomic performance was linked to the degree of centralisation of collective bargaining. Those economies with highly centralised bargaining, such as the Nordic economies with high unionisation rates, were associated with low unemployment – but so also were the economies with highly decentralised bargaining and lower unionisation, such as the US. 'Intermediate' economies, which were neither strongly centralised or strongly decentralised, fared worse and faced higher unemployment. More recent evidence (Pastore and Shorman 2018) has shown that there has been a gradual movement across the board towards decentralisation, but that it is still possible to discern the relationship which Calmfors and Driffill suggested.

The point is that, though in principle both centralised and decentralised systems could produce similar macroeconomic results, the centralised system is associated with greater equality and thus appeals to the Left. However, whether a revival of sectoral bargaining can now be engineered by government is doubtful. The growth of industry- or sector-wide bargaining in the UK was an organic growth: employers developed sectoral representation as a response to the growth of powerful industrial or sectoral unions. The conditions which gave rise to it – economies of scale in heavy productive and extractive industries, similar technologies and working conditions within a national economy – gradually disappeared as we moved towards service-related activities, as economies globalised, supply chains lengthened and ownership shifted abroad, often into conglomerate businesses. National sectoral bargaining thus lost its rationale. The practicalities of putting it back together, through government-created Sectoral Councils, seem likely to prove insuperable in general, though it is possible this could succeed in sectors without significant penetration from foreign-owned businesses. It has been suggested that social care might fit the bill, and Labour has proposed beginning with this sector. However, the small scale of many operators presents another set of problems and we might end up with something like the old Wages Councils rather than the genuine sectoral collective bargaining which the IPPR envisages.[2]

Another proposal put forward by the IPPR Commission, and elaborated on in Dromey's paper, is that 'public and private companies of more than 250 employees should have at least two workers, elected by the workforce, on their main board.' As Dromey admitted, these 'would often be union representatives'. Back in the mid 1970s, the Bullock Committee, set up by Labour as part of the discussions around the Social Contract, had recommended something similar. Though endorsed by the TUC, its conclusions were opposed at the time by many leading unionists (and by Hugh Clegg, who saw them as compromising union independence). They were never implemented. Now, however, worker representation on boards seems more popular on the Left. The advantages claimed for it are fairly nebulous: an 'opportunity for worker voice at the firm level, and for social partnership'.

How this would work out in practice is unclear. In Germany, they have had workers on supervisory boards

---

2   https://capx.co/labours-social-care-plans-are-a-century-out-of-date/

for many decades. In a frequently quoted study of 'co-determination' Gorton and Schmid (2004), looking at the shock associated with restructuring in the wake of German reunification, claim that employees on boards redistribute the firm's surplus towards themselves and reduce shareholder value. Shareholder representatives respond to lower dividends by higher leverage, which commits more cash to leave the firm. This may increase risk to the enterprise's future. A recent study (Jäger et al. 2022) takes a more sympathetic view; however, it finds that co-determination has little impact one way or another. It may possibly cause a marginal increase in wages and job security, but has largely zero or at best small positive effects on firm performance.

Not all the IPPR's proposals are likely to be picked up by the new Labour government, but the party's Deputy Leader, Angela Rayner, has outlined a New Deal[3] which would boost unions. In a speech[4] to the September 2023 TUC conference, she listed a range of measures which Labour intends to introduce. Some of these, such as a higher National Living Wage, higher sickness benefits, 'fair pay' for care workers and a ban on some types of zero-hours contracts, do not directly involve the unions – and indeed, as discussed earlier, might to some extent serve as substitutes for union membership and activism.

---

3   This refers to the Green Paper published by the Labour Party in 2022 (https://labour.org.uk/wp-content/uploads/2022/10/New-Deal-for-Working-People-Green-Paper.pdf).

4   https://www.tuc.org.uk/speeches/deputy-labour-leader-angela-rayners-speech-tuc-congress-2023

But in an Employment Rights Bill promised within the new government's first 100 days, the 2016 Trade Union Act and the 2023 Minimum Service Levels Act will be repealed, a key demand of the unions. And Labour wants to introduce electronic voting in union ballots, to replace postal ballots.

These changes could lead to a few more votes in favour of strike action, although their effects should not be exaggerated; many felt that the 2016 and 2023 legislation was performative rather than effective. Proposals for strong union action have usually been endorsed by ballots in recent disputes despite the hurdles erected by the 2016 legislation, while the minimum service levels law has not so far been used.

One of the recommendations of the IPPR Commission was to give unions access to workplaces to recruit members, and Ms Rayner endorsed this in her TUC speech, though there have so far been no details about how this would operate.

Labour also plans to end the 'fire and rehire' option,[5] by which businesses can, *in extremis*, dismiss workers and then rehire them at lower wage rates.[6] This possibility has rarely been used, so legislation is unlikely to have much impact – although it is yet another restriction on

---

5   https://www.theguardian.com/politics/article/2024/may/08/labour-vows -to-ban-fire-and-rehire-after-war-of-words-with-unions#:~:text=Lab our%20has%20vowed%20it%20will,its%20pledges%20on%20workers'%20 rights

6   Although it was not strictly 'fire and rehire', the dismissal of RMT members by P&O Ferries in 2022 provoked outrage (Shackleton 2022).

employers which might in some circumstances lead to businesses folding and jobs being lost. Additionally, the party intends to make the union recognition process easier, and to strengthen further the law against 'blacklisting' of union activists by employers.[7]

Several of the Labour proposals are rather backward-looking, none perhaps more so than the promise of an enquiry into the violent incidents at Orgreave colliery during the miners' strike forty years ago. Many unionists still believe that Orgreave saw excessive use of force by the police, though it's unclear what useful purpose an inevitably long-drawn-out enquiry could serve at this distance of time.

While the promised reforms may make the work of union officials rather easier, it doesn't seem likely that there will be a marked recovery in union membership as a consequence of such measures; nor that there will be a marked increase in strikes in the private sector. As Ms Rayner notes, some of these measures would replicate conditions found in comparator countries, but these countries have also experienced declining union density and lower levels of strike activity than in the past.

The Labour Party's package of proposals does not seem to involve a rethinking of modern employment challenges, but depends perhaps rather too much on a sentimental attachment to the past of a trade union movement which is

---

7   This harks back to the practice of the Consulting Association, which for many years maintained a database of activists in the construction industry. Following exposure of this practice, there was a Parliamentary enquiry, legislation and a compensation scheme which paid out many millions in redress.

not always all it claims to be. While it may well continue to generate a wage premium and other advantages to some relatively privileged workers – although these gains are declining in importance – the trade union movement is unlikely to be an effective vehicle for the pursuit of the sort of 'economic justice' for the disadvantaged which its champions want to see. Moreover, the suggestion (Dromey 2018: 10) that having more powerful unions would significantly contribute to the higher productivity on which the country's prosperity ultimately rests remains highly contestable.

Classical liberalism and the unions

If the unions and the Labour Party want to try to revive trade unionism by changing the law, is there an argument against this other than a pragmatic assertion that it won't have the benefits union supporters expect? Indeed, is there perhaps even a case for further reducing the influence of unions? One answer might be to look again at the approach of classical liberalism to trade unionism which, while unlikely to appeal to union activists, is worth reexamining.

Modern classical liberal discussion of unions begins with the approach of W. H. Hutt, whose thinking developed in the 1920s and 1930s. His short book *The Theory of Collective Bargaining* (1954) encapsulates his approach. As Ludwig von Mises writes in a preface (p. 11) to the essay, it is

a critical analysis of the arguments advanced by economists from Adam Smith down and by the spokesmen of the unions in favor of the thesis that unionism can raise

> wage rates above the market level without harm to any-
> body else than the 'exploiters.'

As mentioned in chapter 1, Hutt is critical of Adam Smith's belief that workers inevitably face tacit combinations or cartels of employers which can force down wages, or are more generally disadvantaged in the labour market. Smith himself was ambivalent about whether this supposed disadvantage could be offset by collective bargaining. Many economists in the early nineteenth century argued that it could not do so by citing the Wages Fund theory – the belief that capitalists had a fixed fund out of which wages were paid, and unions 'could not affect the size of this fund and hence all efforts to raise the general level of wages were futile' (ibid.: 22). However, the abandonment of the Wages Fund doctrine did not mean that those advocating collective bargaining were right to assume that this could increase labour's share. As Edwin Cannan[8] put it (quoted in Hutt 1954: 30):

> Modern doctrine teaches plainly enough that combina-
> tions of earners can only raise earnings if they can raise
> the value or quantity of the product.

For Hutt, gains by one union, based on its monopoly power over the supply of labour, could only be at the expense of some other group. This might be displaced workers forced to take lower-paying employment, but Hutt also points to

---

8 Edwin Cannan (1861–1935) taught at the London School of Economics. Sympathetic to classical liberalism, he also sided with Alfred Marshall in some matters despite occasional squabbles.

the possibility of a monopoly union colluding with a monopoly producer to keep out competition and so raising prices to the consumer.

By attempting to fix wages, unions prevent the labour market from adjusting optimally to changes in demand and supply. The ultimate gains of trade unions are thus obtained 'either by the "exploitation" of the consumer or the exclusion of competitors (although in the latter case, of course, the consumer also loses)' (ibid.: 143–44).

F. A. Hayek is the best-known twentieth-century exponent of classical liberalism. Hayek knew Hutt, and was on friendly terms with him. His views on the economic effects of unions and collective bargaining were influenced by those of Hutt, but by the time he was writing in the postwar period of rising union power, Hayek went further in his criticisms. While Hutt's analysis was mainly based on a priori reasoning, Hayek sometimes draws, maybe too readily, on casual empirical assertions which may or may not be correct, for instance, in relation to the causes of unemployment and to the effects of unions in sparking an inflationary process which is then validated by monetary expansion (Richardson 1993).

However, Hayek's position is not simply about the economic effects of unions. In *The Constitution of Liberty* (Hayek 1960), it is much more fundamentally about the rule of law, and the way in which the 1906 Trade Disputes Act's granting of immunity from actions for tort, touched on in earlier chapters, has allowed unions to use coercion to pursue their goals (Richardson 1996). A similar line has been taken more recently in the US context by the legal economist Richard Epstein (2013). He abhors the way in which, in a similar manner to Britain, the common law on breach of contract was overridden in the US by the 1935 National Labor Relations Act. He regards unions, quoting the title of his 2013 article, as 'scourges' rather than 'saviors' which in aggregate damage workers rather than benefit them.[9]

Union coercion is 'contrary to all principles of freedom under the law' and it is 'primarily the coercion of fellow workers' (Hayek 2009: 78). Three aspects are mentioned. First, unions are said to rely on the use of the picket line as an 'instrument of intimidation' (ibid.: 85):

> That even so-called 'peaceful' picketing in numbers is severely coercive and the condoning of it constitutes a privilege conceded because of its presumed legitimate aim is shown by the fact that it can be used by persons who themselves are not workers to force others to form a union which they will control.

This issue of picketing is also stressed by Epstein (2013: 12), although he concedes that some picketing could serve an informational rather than coercive function. These functions are difficult to separate in practice, however.

9　He writes (Epstein 2013: 8) that 'nothing ... justifies the extraordinary set of legal privileges that they have received over the past 100 years' and considers the decline of unions in the US to be an 'unalloyed good which contributes to the overall health of the American labor markets'. He believes that 'no raft of well-crafted union organization campaigns could return unions to their glory days' (ibid.: 30).

Second, Hayek points to the 'closed or union shop and its varieties' – which require, remember, that workers must belong to a union in order to be employed by a particular business or organisation. Closed shops 'constitute contracts in restraint of trade' and only their exemption from the ordinary rules of law allowed unions and employers to impose them (ibid.: 86).[10]

Finally, 'all secondary strikes and boycotts which are used ... as a means of forcing other workers to fall in with union policies' (ibid.).

Hayek makes it clear that he has no objection in principle to the existence of unions: 'it would be contrary to all our principles even to consider the possibility of prohibiting them altogether' (ibid.: 87). As properly voluntary and non-coercive institutions, which have spontaneously arisen without state involvement, unions clearly have a place in a free society, and 'they may have important services to render'. Although in his analysis unions would no longer have the power significantly to alter the overall pattern of wages and employment, they might still have a role in the process of wage determination, for example (on Freeman and Medoff lines) in pushing for workers' preferences for alternative benefits which could be provided at the same cost as pay increases, or in helping determine the appropriate pattern of pay differentials, grievance procedures and other rules within the organisation (ibid.: 89). He is also keen on the 'friendly society' role of unions, 'a highly

---

10 For an impression of the widespread concern over the closed shop in the 1970s, see Burton (1978).

desirable form of self-help'. He draws the line, however, at German-style 'codetermination', arguing that businesses cannot be conducted in the interest of workers at the same time as serving the interest of consumers.

Hayek is quite explicit in saying what is necessary in order to return unions to legitimacy: the prohibition of coercive picketing and the banning of closed shops. Such reforms would also tend to render ineffective secondary strikes and boycotts.

Writing in the 1960s and 1970s, Hayek was gloomy about the prospects for reform. But as we saw in chapter 4, the Thatcher and Major governments carried out more or less exactly what he proposed: closed shops, mass picketing and secondary strikes were all banned, and remain so. The Labour Party has no plans to change this. Hayek said nothing in *The Constitution of Liberty* about prohibiting strikes or employer recognition of unions or rules about balloting (which he would probably regard as the unions' own responsibility). As we have seen, in the heightened atmosphere of 1970s militancy, he called for repeal of the Trade Disputes Act, but his own analysis suggests that strikes (whether protected against tort or not) would probably be ineffective without union power to coerce.

So perhaps, contrary to preconceptions, we have been living for the last thirty years in an industrial relations environment which Hayek would have tolerated or even more or less approved? It's an interesting question. While there may be much room for improvement within the UK labour market, critics from the Right might argue that there is now more of a problem of excessive and ill-understood government regulation[11] than of the over-mighty union-ism of which Hayek complained.

Be that as it may, does the recent outbreak of strike ac-tivity suggest that we have become too complacent, and that Britain could rather easily slip back into a period of almost constant strike activity, albeit on a smaller scale than in the 1970s?

If that were to be the case, there might eventually be pressure for government action to mitigate the damage to the public, which in modern conditions is the primary objective of many if not most strikes, particularly in the public sector. This pressure would even affect a Sir Keir Starmer–led government, just as it was felt by Starmer's predecessors Harold Wilson, James Callaghan and their colleagues in the 1960s and 1970s.

Arbitration, conciliation and reform of collective bargaining

What might be the response? One possibility would be to move in the direction of greater government intervention in industrial disputes, even to compulsory arbitration where appropriate. New Zealand set an example as early as 1896 by banning strikes and lockouts and setting up a

---

11 It can of course be argued that much of this regulation came about through the political pressure which unions have been able to exercise through their links to the Labour Party (at both national and local authority level), although much of it came from the European Union while we were mem-bers, and from the coalition and Conservative governments since 2010 (Shackleton 2017: 230–33).

special court of arbitration, presided over by a judge. For a time the country was known as 'the land without strikes' (Phelps Brown 1983: 48). Although nowadays strikes are legal in New Zealand under certain conditions, these conditions are a great deal tighter than in the UK. Similarly Australia took arbitration powers early in the twentieth century, though their form has changed many times and there are some differences between the country's states (ibid.: ch. 14). Although strikes continue to occur, nowadays the country's Fair Work Commission (FWC) lays down restrictive criteria for what is a legitimate strike, and can declare illegal those strikes which breach these rules. Moreover, if the parties to a dispute cannot agree, the FWC has the power to make binding 'workplace determinations', in other words impose an agreement on the parties.

The FWC, and the appropriate minister, also have powers to ban industrial action which could inflict significant damage to the Australian economy or threatens to endanger the welfare of the population. This power has been used to force Monash University academics to go back to work to produce exam results, and to ban a proposed strike by Sydney Trains employees (McCrystal 2019: 138).

Such regulatory intervention is clearly very different from the UK's tradition of voluntarism. However, there was once considerable interest in some quarters in following the New Zealand example. As early as 1893, the Labour Department of the Board of Trade had intervened in an attempt to secure a settlement of a bitter and violent dispute between miners and employers (Brodie 2003: 58). And in 1896 a Conciliation Act was passed, with the government setting up a voluntary conciliation and arbitration ser-vice,[12] the forerunner of today's ACAS.

Weaker unions sometimes wanted to go further, feeling that that they might get a better deal through compulsory arbitration than through prolonged industrial action. For eight years in succession a motion was tabled at the TUC annual conference proposing compulsory arbitration. This idea also strongly appealed to that doughty champion of trade unionism, Sidney Webb. In a memorandum ap-pended to the Royal Commission set up after the Taff Vale judgement, he wrote that (quoted in Phelps Brown 1983: 49):

> A strike or a lock-out ... necessarily involves so much dislocation of industry; so much individual suffering; so much injury to third parties, and so much national loss, that it cannot, in my opinion, be accepted as the normal way of settling an intractable dispute ... The various in-dustrial conciliation and arbitration laws of New Zea-land and Australia ... offer, to the general satisfaction of employers and employed, both a guarantee against con-ditions of employment that are demonstrably injurious to the community as a whole, and an effective remedy for industrial war.

Nothing came of this. But there have been occasions when the British state has taken a more active role (Beaumont

---

12 There had previously been some examples of privately arranged Boards of Conciliation, or Conciliation and Arbitration (Phelps Brown 1983: 106).

1982). During World War I, the Munitions of War Acts provided for legally binding arbitration in disputes which could not otherwise be resolved. Between the wars, the Industrial Courts Act of 1919 created a permanent arbitration tribunal, the Industrial Court, which arbitrated disputes at the request of unions and employers, though it had no powers of compulsion. During World War II, the Conditions of Employment and National Arbitration Order 1305 of 1940 gave the government apparently extensive powers, although relatively few attempts were in practice made to enforce the law against striking (ibid.: 323). It does, however, seem to have encouraged conciliation of disputes.

Order 1305 was to remain in force until 1951, when it was replaced by Industrial Disputes Order 1376. This continued in operation until 1959; during the eight years of its operation, the Industrial Disputes Tribunal made 1,277 awards under the terms of the Order.

After this, the emphasis on voluntarism which dominated industrial relations thinking in the 1960s meant that all political parties preferred to allow unions and employers to reach agreements under their own steam, with conciliation and arbitration purely private options. The attempt by the Heath government to break with this consensus and the introduction (in the Industrial Relations Act of 1971) of powers to intervene in disputes by imposing cooling-off periods and compulsory ballots during a dispute proved unsuccessful. At a time when the government was operating a formal incomes policy, it was very difficult to combine imposing wage restraint with being seen as an honest broker in industrial disputes.

Following the demise of the Heath administration, successive governments have shied away from direct involvement in disputes. As part of this, responsibility for conciliation and (voluntary) arbitration was hived off from the then Department of Employment to ACAS, the independent Advisory, Conciliation and Arbitration Service. This was set up in September 1974 and given clear terms of reference the following year. It was to provide conciliation and mediation and, where necessary, facilities for arbitration.[13] Independence from government direction was spelt out in the Employment Protection Act 1975 (Sisson and Taylor 2006).

In the almost half-century since it began, ACAS has become part of the landscape. It has changed considerably, however, with the bulk of its activity now focused on individuals' grievances (all 100,000-plus annual applications to employment tribunals must first involve complainants having worked with ACAS to see if their claims can be conciliated). It also has a major role in providing guidance and advice to employers and unions, and promulgates codes of practice on such matters as disciplinary procedures, information disclosure and flexible working.[14]

It does, however, still have a significant involvement in conciliating disputes between employers and unions. In the year to March 2023, for example, its services were requested to help resolve 621 collective disputes, with a

---

13 At the time, it was also given a remit to promote the extension of collective bargaining. The Conservatives removed this statutory duty in 1993.

14 These codes of practice are used as a benchmark by employment tribunals in considering cases.

claimed success rate of 91%.[15] An ACAS analysis covering the period immediately before Covid (Urwin 2020) estimated that the organisation's conciliation activities produced a benefit of £93 million in a full year as a result of strike days avoided.

While we shouldn't downplay the benefits of these conciliation activities, some disputes are seemingly intractable and it is in these cases that there might be an argument for powers to impose binding arbitration at some stage in a dispute. Perhaps this might be after so many working days have been lost or where the government decides, on Australian lines, that the costs to third parties such as NHS patients or schoolchildren are disproportionate to any potential benefits to the strikers. Arbitration would be difficult to impose in public sector strikes which are currently seen as direct confrontations to government policy, but this has been done in other countries.[16] It would be facilitated if we moved away from the government being a monolithic employer and allow different parts of the public sector more autonomy in pay-setting, subject of course to budgetary control.

---

15 See ACAS annual report (https://assets.publishing.service.gov.uk/govern ment/uploads/system/uploads/attachment_data/file/1170207/advisory -conciliation-and-arbitration-service-acas-annual-report-and-accounts -2022-to-20223-accessible.pdf).

16 In recent decades, Final Offer Arbitration has become popular in public sector disputes in many countries. Introduced originally in the US and Canada in the police and fire services, it involves the arbitrator having to choose between the final offers of parties to the dispute rather than splitting the difference. It is said to motivate each party to negotiate realistically.

Government pay arrangements are indeed a confusing and illogical mess, varying widely across the public sector (Brione and Francis-Devine 2022). Pay awards for about 45% of public employees – including the armed forces, the police, teachers, the Senior Civil Service and the NHS – are decided by ministers and based on the recommendation of eight Pay Review Bodies, the earliest of which dates back to 1960. Awards for the Civil Service are decided by individual departments which, however, are allowed to vary very little from 'guidance' issued by the Cabinet Office. Pay for local government workers, on the other hand, is agreed in more traditional negotiations between employers and trade unions through the National Joint Council for Local Government Services, set up decades ago. For devolved public sector bodies, pay policy is set by the devolved administrations.

Another way to deal with the problems of public sector industrial relations could involve abandoning the cumbersome and time-consuming system of pay reviews, which are constrained by government policies on pay pauses and caps, and have lost whatever credibility they once had. In any case, with the best will in the world, it's difficult to see what sense the NHS Agenda for Change Pay Review Body, which is supposed to set pay for hundreds of different roles in a workforce considerably larger than the population of Birmingham, can make of its annual task.

Long-running and damaging disputes might be relieved by abandoning national collective bargaining and disaggregating large concentrations of public sector employment. We have seen, for example, that Scotland has been able to settle some NHS disputes by making its own deals independently from the rest of the country. Before Covid, the separate Train Operating Companies made their own arrangements with unions, and although there were many tiresome strikes in individual franchises, there was no possibility of a national strike.

Apart from the reduction of national disputes, more disaggregated public sector pay settlements would help the labour market work more flexibility. If some teachers or nurses could more easily be paid extra in areas and specialisms of scarcity, without increasing pay across the board, there would be fewer teacher or nurse shortages and probably lower overall budgetary costs.

Unions in the private sector are inevitably forced to make concessions to market forces, but our public sector pay arrangements perpetuate union restrictions which can damage flexibility and productivity.

Strike bans?

If seriously damaging public sector strikes cannot be avoided through conciliation and reforms to pay arrangements, and compulsory arbitration is not thought feasible, another possibility to consider is outright strike bans in some areas.

The Conservatives had long argued that strikes in areas such as transport, the health service, fire and rescue, education and others create such potential problems for the public that there should be special arrangements made to provide minimum service levels during strikes. The

Strikes (Minimum Service Levels) Act became law in 2023. However, in a particular dispute it would involve quickly consulting the unions and other relevant parties, conducting a risk assessment, determining an adequate minimum standard, defining who is to provide it and what sanctions could be implemented for non-compliance. In what has so far been the only attempt to use the legislation, the government-owned railway company LNER backed down when ASLEF, the train drivers' union, threatened additional strikes.[17] As indicated earlier, this legislation is in line for repeal under a Labour government.

In any case, it might be simpler to avoid the strike completely. In principle, a no-strike agreement could be reached voluntarily, with unions agreeing not to strike in return for higher pay or other benefits than they would otherwise gain. Few unions in Britain would currently contemplate such a deal, but this may change. The Royal College of Nursing had a de facto arrangement to avoid strikes, but abandoned it. When Boris Johnson was London mayor he tried to get a no-strike deal with London Underground workers, but failed. He then called for legislation to impose a ban on strikes and recourse to compulsory arbitration of pay claims. He did not, however, take the opportunity to pursue this proposal when he was in government.

An outright ban on striking is unusual in the UK context. The armed forces cannot strike, as is the case in most countries. Nor, since 1919, can the police strike. And nor

17 Train drivers call off extra strike days after LNER minimum service law U-turn. *The Guardian* (https://www.theguardian.com/business/2024/jan/22/train-drivers-extra-strike-lner-aslef).

can prison officers, a prohibition which was confirmed in the High Court as recently as 2017.

It is often asserted that strike bans, or even the more modest minimum services agreement requirement, are in breach of International Labor Organization rules. But this is not so. A decision of the ILO's Committee on Freedom of Association states:

> Compulsory arbitration to end a collective labour dispute and a strike is acceptable if it is at the request of both parties involved in a dispute, or if the strike in question may be restricted, even banned, i.e. in the case of disputes in the public service involving public servants exercising authority in the name of the State or in essential services in the strict sense of the term, namely those services whose interruption would endanger the life, personal safety or health of the whole or part of the population.[18]

Although the wording could be simpler, this paragraph justifies any number of strike bans, as 'public servants exercising authority in the name of the State' and 'services whose interruption would endanger life, personal safety or health' together cover many possibilities.

Certainly, bans on strikes in some ILO-compliant countries go far beyond the narrow range of employment covered in the UK. In Germany, for example, civil servants – defined to include university staff and many

---

18 https://www.ilo.org/dyn/normlex/en/f?p=NORMLEXPUB:70002:0::NO::P
70002_HIER_ELEMENT_ID,P70002_HIER_LEVEL:3945625,2

teachers – are prohibited from striking. The same goes for some categories of Danish civil servants. People working in public utilities and health and social care, air traffic controllers, fire and rescue workers, and some telecommunications employees can't strike in Czechia and Slovakia. In Poland many civil service and other government officials are banned from striking. The same applies in Estonia, where rescue workers are also prohibited from strike action.[19]

Meanwhile, in the US strike bans are considerably more far-reaching. No federal employee is allowed to strike, assert the right to strike, or belong to a union that 'asserts the right to strike against the government of the United States.' It is even a felony to strike against the US or belong to a union that asserts the right to strike against the US. The Office of Personnel Management can declare an individual who participates in a strike unsuitable for federal employment forever afterwards.[20]

There was the famous occasion in 1981 when 13,000 air-traffic controllers went on strike and President Reagan, after declaring the strike a 'peril to national safety', ordered them back to work. When they refused to comply they were all sacked. Memory of this event means that, even when Congress stops all funding to the government and federal staff go unpaid – as has happened more than once – people keep on working.

---

19 https://tinyurl.com/yrzwa4wp

20 https://www.govexec.com/management/2019/01/why-feds-dont-strike/
    154438/

And of course it is not just federal employees. The states often have prohibitions against strikes by public employees. For example, public school teachers cannot strike in Georgia, North and South Carolina, Texas and Virginia.

These may be more extreme examples than are ever likely to be implemented in the UK. Nevertheless it is possible to conceive of pressure for extending restrictions on the right to strike if, for instance, disputes in the NHS (such as that of the junior doctors) continued indefinitely without resolution. This would be politically difficult under a Labour administration, but stranger things have happened.

Conclusion

There is little prospect of a significant spontaneous recovery in the membership numbers of the UK's trade union movement, certainly in its traditional form. While it might be that a repeal of some existing 'anti-union' legislation, plus the introduction of government incentives to union recognition, could lead to small increases in unionisation, the changes which have taken place in the working population's occupations, skills, qualifications, attitudes and lifestyles render a return to union density levels of the 1970s and 1980s extremely unlikely.

Even were a government-incentivised expansion of union membership possible, the arguments for such an intervention are weak. The benefits which union membership provides are, in twenty-first-century conditions, limited and falling. These gains may very often be at the expense of other participants in the economy, be they non-union workers, shareholders, consumers or, increasingly, taxpayers. It is fallacious to argue that, because some union members may gain from their membership, mass union membership would benefit everybody. Unions impose costs in terms of slower adjustment to economic change and thus slower productivity growth.

But if there is no strong case for expanding union membership, there is no strong argument either for suppressing unions. It may be true that immunity against tort action privileges trade unions, but an equivalent privilege is common throughout the Western world in one form or another, and is not something which any significant grouping wants to remove. As we have noted, the major problem identified by Hayek in the 1960s and 1970s was the ability of unions to achieve their goals through coercion. That has now largely disappeared. There can be no objection in principle to voluntary trade union membership, particularly if unions can evolve into organisations which build on 'friendly society' activities which reach out to disadvantaged workers.

Within the private sector, large-scale long-running disputes have become uncommon. Private sector strikes, as in the Hicks model discussed in chapter 5, are now largely self-limiting as unions have been deprived of the coercive powers they accumulated in the early post-war period. Ultimately, both the employer and the union have a common interest in keeping the business going. Where significant strikes still occur, it is because of the residual involvement of government in what were meant to be privatised enterprises: the Department of Transport's hold on the railways' purse-strings since the collapse of the franchise system, or the continuing importance of the Universal Service Obligation for Royal Mail.

So it is in the public sector where the real core of the recent outbreak of strikes lies. Most people have few alternatives to the service provided by the state in healthcare or education, and none at all in the case of passport provision, driving licences or street cleaning. This gives unions the ability to punish the public in an attempt to extort higher pay from the government, which ultimately means the taxpayer. It is difficult to offer a defensible rationale for such a power in modern conditions in a democratic country. If we are to see a reversion to regular and prolonged strike activity in key parts of the public sector, it seems likely that sooner or later responsible governments of any political persuasion will have to take action to restrict or abolish this power.

REFERENCES

Abel, W., Tenreyro, S. and Thwaites, G. (eds) (2018) Monopsony in the UK. CEPR Press Discussion Paper 13265 (https://cepr.org/publications/dp13265).

Ackers, P. (2007) Collective bargaining as industrial democracy: Hugh Clegg and the political foundations of British industrial relations pluralism. *British Journal of Industrial Relations* 45(1): 77–101.

Addison, J. T. (2020) The consequences of trade union power erosion. *IZA World of Labor* 2020: 68v2.

Addison, J. T. and Belfield, C. R. (2004) Unions and employment growth: the one constant? *Industrial Relations* 43(2): 305–23.

Baroda, N. (2021) 'Enoch was right?' The Left and Enoch Powell. *Webster Review of International History* 1(1): 45–64.

Barth, E., Bryson, A. and Dale-Olsen, H. (2020a) Union density effects on productivity and wages. *Economic Journal* 130(631): 1898–936.

Barth, E., Bryson, A. and Dale-Olsen, H. (2020b) Do public subsidies of union membership increase union membership rates? IZA Discussion Paper 13747.

Baumol, W. J. (2012) *The Cost Disease: Why Computers Get Cheaper and Health Care Doesn't.* New Haven, CT: Yale University Press.

Bessa, I., Charlwood, A. and Valizade, D. (2020) Do unions cause job dissatisfaction? Evidence from a quasi-experiment in the

United Kingdom. *British Journal of Industrial Relations* 59(2): 251–78.

Beaumont, P. B. (1982) Dispute resolution and arbitration in Britain: current trends and prospects. *Case Western Reserve Journal of International Law* 14(2): 323–38.

Blanchflower, D. and Bryson, A. (2008) Union decline in Britain. CEP Discussion Paper 864 (https://cep.lse.ac.uk/pubs/down load/dp0864.pdf).

Blanchflower, D. and Bryson, A. (2010) The wage impact of trade unions in the UK public and private sectors. *Economica* 77(305): 92–109.

Blanchflower, D., Millward, N. and Oswald, A. (1991) Unionism and employment behaviour. *Economic Journal* 101: 815–34.

Blanchflower, D., Bryson, A. and Green, C. (2022) Trade unions and the well-being of workers. *British Journal of Industrial Relations* 60(2): 255–77.

Booth, A. L. (1985) The free rider problem and a social custom model of trade union membership. *Quarterly Journal of Economics* 100(1): 253–61.

Booth, A. L. (1995) *The Economics of the Trade Union.* Cambridge University Press.

Borjas, G. J. (1979) Job satisfaction, wages, and unions. *Journal of Human Resources* XIV(1): 21–40.

Borjas, G. J. (2013) *Labor Economics*, 6th edn. New York: McGraw Hill.

Brändle, T. and Goerke, L. (2015) The one constant: a causal effect of collective bargaining on employment growth? Evidence from German linked-employer-employee data. IAW Discussion Papers 116, Institut für Angewandte Wirtschaftsforschung (IAW).

Brione, P. and Francis-Devine, B. (2022) Public sector pay. House of Commons Library Briefing Paper 8037.

Brittan, S. (1979) The futility of British incomes policy. *Challenge* 22(2): 5–13.

Brodie, D. (2003) *A History of British Labour Law 1867–1945.* Oxford and Portland, OR: Hart Publishing.

Bryson, A. (2004) Unions and employment growth in British workplaces during the 1990s: a panel analysis. *Scottish Journal of Political Economy* 51(4): 477–506.

Bryson, A. (2007) The effects of trade unions on wages. *Reflets et Perspectives de la Vie Economique* XLVI(2/3): 33–45.

Bryson, A. (2014) Union wage effects. *IZA World of Labor* 2014: 35.

Bryson, A. and Forth, J. (2011) Trade unions. In *The Labour Market in Winter: The State of Working Britain* (ed. P. Gregg and J. Wadsworth). Oxford University Press.

Bryson, A. and Forth, J. (2017) *The Added Value of Trade Unions.* London: TUC.

Bryson, A. and Willman, P. (2022) How should we think about employers' associations? *British Journal of Industrial Relations* Special Issue 1-13.

Bryson, A., Willman, P., Gomez, R. and Kretschner, T. (2013) The comparative advantage of non-union voice in Britain 1980–2004. *Industrial Relations* 52(S1): 194–220.

Bryson, A., Freeman, R. B., Gomez, R. and Willman, P. (2017) The twin track model of employee voice: an Anglo-American perspective on union decline and the rise of alternative forms of voice. IZA Discussion Paper 11223.

Bryson, A., Dale-Olsen, H. and Nergaard, K. (2019) Gender differences in the union wage premium? A comparative case study. *European Journal of Industrial Relations* 26(2): 173–90.

Buchmueller, T. C., DiNardo, J. E. and Valletta, R. G (2004) A sub-merging labor market institution? Unions and the nonwage aspects of work. In *Emerging Labour Market Institutions for the Twenty-First Century* (ed. R. Freeman, J. Hersch and L. Mishel). Chicago University Press.

Burke, T. and Field, A. (2023) *A Glorious History: Print and Paper-making Unions in the UK*. London: Unite the Union.

Burton, J. (1978) Are trade unions a public good/'bad': the eco-nomics of the closed shop. In *Trade Unions: Public Goods or Public 'Bads'?*, IEA Readings 17. London: Institute of Economic Affairs

Calmfors, L. and Driffill, J. (1988) Bargaining structure, corpo-ratism and macroeconomic performance. *Economic Policy* 3(6): 13–61.

Card, D., Lemieux, T. and Riddell, W. C. (2018) Unions and wage inequality: the roles of gender, skill and public sector employ-ment. IZA Discussion Paper 11964.

Certification Officer (2020) Applying to have the name of an or-ganisation entered in the Certification Officer's list of trade unions. Guidance on making an application to the Certifica-tion Office to enter a trade union on the Certification Officer's list of trade unions (https://www.gov.uk/guidance/apply-to-enter-a-trade-union-on-the-certification-officers-list).

Clegg, H. A. (1960) *A New Approach to Industrial Democracy*. Ox-ford: Blackwell.

Cominetti, N., Costa, R., Eyles, A., Moev, T. and Ventura, G. (2022) *Changing Jobs? Changes in the UK Labour Market and the Role of Labour Mobility*. London: Resolution Foundation.

DDCMS (2021) Platinum Jubilee weekend 2022. Impact assess-ment. RPC Reference RPC-DCMS-5045(1) (https://assets.pub

lishing.service.gov.uk/government/uploads/system/uploads/attachment_data/file/1057164/Platinum_Jubilee_Impact_Assessment__web_accessible_.pdf).

Demougin, P., Gooberman, L., Hauptmeier, M. and Heery, E. (2019) Employer organisations transformed. *Human Resource Management Journal* 29(1): 1–16.

DfT (2023) Rail strikes: understanding the impact on passengers – summary findings. Research and analysis (https://www.gov.uk/government/publications/rail-strikes-understanding-the-impact-on-passengers/rail-strikes-understanding-the-impact-on-passengers-summary-findings#key-findings).

Dodini, S., Salvanes, K. and Willén, A. (2021) The dynamics of power in labor markets: monopolistic unions versus monopolistic employers. CESifo Working Paper 9495.

Dorey, P. (2009) *British Conservatism and Trade Unionism, 1945–1964.* Farnham: Ashgate.

Doucouliagos, C. and Laroche, P. (2003) What do unions do to productivity? A meta-analysis. *Industrial Relations* 42(4): 650–90.

Doucouliagos, H., Freeman, R. B. and Laroche, P. (2017) *The Economics of Trade Unions: A Study of a Research Field and Its Findings.* Abingdon: Routledge.

Downing, A. (2013) The Sheffield outrages: violence, class and trade unionism, 1850–1870. *Social History* 38(2): 162–82.

Dromey, J. (2018) Power to the people: how stronger unions can deliver economic justice. IPPR Commission Discussion Paper (https://www.ippr.org/files/2018-06/cej-trade-unions-may18-.pdf).

Duffy, A. E. P. (1961) New unionism in Britain, 1889–1890: a reappraisal. *Economic History Review* 14(2): 306–19.

Edgerton, D. (2019) *The Rise and Fall of the British Nation: A Twentieth-Century History.* Harmondsworth: Penguin.

Elvira, M. M. and Saporta, I. (2001) How does collective bargaining affect the gender pay gap? *Work and Occupations* 28(4): 469–90.

Epstein, R. (1984) In defense of the contract at will. *University of Chicago Law Review* 51(4): 947–82.

Epstein, R. (2012) The deserved demise of EFCA (and why the NLRA should share its fate). In *Research Handbook on the Economics of Labor and Employment Law* (ed. C. L. Estland and M. L. Wachter). Cheltenham: Edward Elgar.

Epstein, R. (2013) Labor unions: saviors or scourges? *Capital University Law Review* 41(1): 1–33.

Fanfani, B. (2023) The employment effects of collective wage bargaining. *Journal of Public Economics* 227: 105006.

Fetter, F. W. (1980) *The Economist in Parliament: 1780–1868.* Durham, NC: Duke University Press.

Flanders, A. (1968) Collective bargaining: a theoretical analysis. *British Journal of Industrial Relations* 6(1): 1–26.

Flanders, A. (1974) The tradition of voluntarism. *British Journal of Industrial Relations* 12(3): 352–70.

Forth, J. and Bryson, A. (2019) State substitution for the trade union good: the case of paid holiday entitlements. *Journal of Participation and Employee Ownership* 2(1): 5–23.

Forth, J., Theodoropoulos, N. and Bryson, A. (2023) The role of the workplace in ethnic wage differentials. *British Journal of Industrial Relations* 61(2): 259–90.

Frangi, L., Zhang, T. and Hebdon, R. (2020) Tweeting and retweeting for fight for $15: unions as dinosaur opinion leaders? *British Journal of Industrial Relations* 58(2): 301–35.

Frank, W. F. (1959) The state and industrial arbitration in the United Kingdom. *Louisiana Law Review* 19(1): 617–42.

Freeman, R. F. (1981) The effect of unionism on fringe benefits. *ILR Review* 34(4): 489–509.

Freeman, R. F. and Medoff, J. L. (1984) *What Do Unions Do?* New York: Basic Books.

Friedman, M. (1962) *Capitalism and Freedom.* Chicago University Press.

Gall, G. (2021) Contemporary employer victimisation of lay union representatives in Britain: issues, dynamics and extent. *Capital and Class* 45(1): 45–70.

Gooberman, L., Hauptmeier, M. and Heery, E. (2019) The decline of employers' associations in the UK, 1976–2014. *Journal of Industrial Relations* 16(1): 11–32.

Gorton, G. and Schmid, F. (2004) Capital, labor and the firm: a study of German codetermination. *Journal of the European Economic Association* 2(5): 863–905.

Gouldstone, S. and Morris, G. (2006) The Central Arbitration Committee. In *The Changing Institutional Face of British Employment Relations* (ed. L. Dickens and A. C. Neal). Alphen aan den Rijn: Kluwer Law International.

Grampp, W. D. (1979) The economists and the Combination Laws. *Quarterly Journal of Economics* 93(4): 501–22.

Groenewegen, P. D. (1994) Alfred Marshall and the Labour Commission 1891–1894. *European Journal of the History of Economic Thought* 1(2): 273–96.

Günther, W. and Höpner, M. (2023) Why does Germany abstain from statutory bargaining extensions? Explaining the exceptional German erosion of collective wage bargaining. *Economic and Industrial Democracy* 44(1): 88–108.

Hayek, F. A. (1960) *The Constitution of Liberty.* University of Chicago Press.

Hayek, F. A. (2009) *A Tiger by the Tail,* 3rd edn, with additional material. London: Institute of Economic Affairs and Ludwig von Mises Institute.

Hicks, J. R. (1963 [1932]) *The Theory of Wages,* 2nd edn. London: Macmillan.

Hipp, L. and Kolins Gavan, R. (2015) What do unions do? A cross-national reexamination of the relationship between unionisation and job satisfaction. *Social Forces* 94(1): 349–77.

Hirsch, B. (1997) Unionization and economic performance: evidence on productivity, profits, investment, and growth. Public Policy Sources 3, Fraser Institute Occasional Paper.

Hirsch, B. (2012) Unions, dynamism, and economic performance. In *Research Handbook on the Economics of Labor and Employment Law* (ed. C. L. Estland and M. L. Wachter). Cheltenham: Edward Elgar.

Hodder, A., Williams, M., Kelly, J. and McCarthy, N. (2017) Does strike action stimulate trade union membership growth? *British Journal of Industrial Relations* 55(1): 165–86.

Hogedahl, L., Nergaard, K. and Alsos, K. (2022) Trade unions in the Nordic labor market models – signs of erosion? Introduction to the Special Issue. *Nordic Journal of Working Life Studies* 12(S8): 1–5.

Hupfel, S. (2022) The economists and the Combination Laws: a reappraisal. *Journal of the History of Economic Thought* 44(1): 72–94.

Hutt, W. H. (1954) *The Theory of Collective Bargaining.* Glencoe, IL: Free Press.

IPPR (2018) *Prosperity and Justice: A Plan for the New Economy.*

Jäger, S., Noy, S. and Schoefer, B. (2022) What does codetermination do? *ILR Review* 75(4): 857–90.

Jenkins, R. (1998) *The Chancellors*. London: Macmillan.

Kynaston, D. (2014) *Modernity Britain Book Two: A Shake of the Dice 1959–62*. London: Bloomsbury.

Landry, J. R. (2016) Fair responses to unfair labor practices: enforcing federal labor law through non-traditional forms of action. *Columbia Law Review* 116(1): 147–94.

Laroche, P. (2016) A meta-analysis of the union-job satisfaction relationship. *British Journal of Industrial Relations* 54(4): 709–41.

Laroche, P. (2017) Research shows unionized workers are less happy, but why? *Harvard Business Review*, 30 August (https://hbr.org/2017/08/research-shows-unionized-workers-are-less-happy-but-why).

Laroche, P. (2020) Unions, collective bargaining and firm performance. Global Labor Organization Discussion Paper 728.

Leonard, J. S. (1992) Unions and employment growth. *Industrial Relations* 31(1): 80–94.

Manning, A. (2003) *Monopsony in Motion: Imperfect Competition in Labor Market*. Princeton University Press.

Marshall, A. (1920) *Principles of Economics*, 8th edn. London: Macmillan.

McCrystal, S. (2019) Why is it so hard to take lawful strike action in Australia? *Journal of Industrial Relations* 61(1): 129–44.

Metcalf, D. (1993) Industrial relations and economic performance. *British Journal of Industrial Relations* 31(June): 255–83.

Moher, J. G. (2009) The Osborne Judgement of 1909: trade union funding of political parties in historical perspective (https://www.historyandpolicy.org/policy-papers/papers/the-os

borne-judgement-of-1909-trade-union-funding-of-political
-parties-in-h).

Moore, C. (2015) *Margaret Thatcher: The Authorized Biography*, vol. 2: *Everything She Wants*. London: Allen Lane.

Morris, M. (1976) *The General Strike*. Harmondsworth: Penguin.

Musgrave, R. (1959) *A Theory of Public Finance*. New York: McGraw-Hill.

National Archives (2019) Early trade unions and the Combination Laws. Records and Research (https://blog.national archives.gov.uk/for-obtaining-an-advance-of-wages-and -for-lessening-the-hours-of-working-early-trade-unions-and -the-combination-laws/).

Niemietz, K. (2019) *Socialism: The Failed Idea That Never Dies*. London: Institute of Economic Affairs.

Olson, M. (1965) *The Logic of Collective Action: Public Goods and the Theory of Groups*. Cambridge, MA: Harvard University Press.

ONS (2023) The impact of strikes in the UK: June 2022 to February 2023 (https://www.ons.gov.uk/employmentandlabour market/peopleinwork/workplacedisputesandworkingcon ditions/articles/theimpactofstrikesintheuk/june2022tofeb ruary2023).

ONS (2024) RPI All Items: Percentage change over 12 months: Jan 1987=100. Source dataset: Consumer price inflation time series (MM23) (https://www.ons.gov.uk/economy/inflation andpriceindices/timeseries/czbh/mm23).

Orth, J. V. (1987) English Combination Acts of the eighteenth century. *Law and History Review* 5(1): 175–211.

Parker, H. M. D. (1957) *Manpower: A Study of Wartime Policy and Administration*. London: HMSO.

Pastore, T. and Shorman, A. (2018) Calmfors and Driffill revisited: analysis of European institutional and macroeconomic heterogeneity. Sciences Po Working Paper 33 (https://www.ofce.sciences-po.fr/pdf/dtravail/OFCEWP201833.pdf).

Pelling, H. (1992) *A History of British Trade Unionism,* 5th edn. Basingstoke: Palgrave Macmillan.

Phelps Brown, H. (1983) *The Origins of Trade Union Power.* Oxford: Clarendon Press.

Pimlott, B. (1992) *Harold Wilson.* London: HarperCollins.

Pyper, D. (2018) Check-off. House of Commons Briefing Paper CBP 7982 (https://researchbriefings.files.parliament.uk/documents/CBP-7982/CBP-7982.pdf).

Richardson, R. (1993) Hayek on trade unions: social philosopher or propagandist? Centre for Economic Performance Discussion Paper 178.

Richardson, R. (1996) Coercion and the trade unions: a reconsideration of Hayek. *British Journal of Industrial Relations* 34(2): 219–36.

Robinson, J. (1933) *The Economics of Imperfect Competition.* London: Macmillan.

Rosen, S. (1969) Trade union power, threat effects and the extent of organization. *Review of Economic Studies* 36: 185–96.

Samuelson, P. (1954) The pure theory of public expenditure. *Review of Economics and IZA World of Labor.*

Sandbrook, D. (2006) *White Heat: A History of Britain in the Swinging Sixties.* London: Abacus.

Sandbrook, D. (2013) *Seasons in the Sun: Britain, 1974–1979.* London: Penguin Random House.

Scarpetta, S. (2014) Employment protection. *IZA World of Labor* 2014.12.

Shackleton, J. R. (1998) Industrial relations reform in Britain since 1979. *Journal of Labor Research* 19: 581–605.

Shackleton, J. R. (2007) Britain's labor market under the Blair governments. *Journal of Labor Research* 28: 454–76.

Shackleton, J. R. (2017) *Working to Rule: The Damaging Economics of UK Employment Regulation.* London: Institute of Economic Affairs.

Shackleton, J. R. (2022) The P&O saga: no way to say goodbye? London: Institute of Economic Affairs (https://iea.org.uk/the -po-saga-no-way-to-say-goodbye/).

Siebert, W. S. and Addison, J. T. (1981) Are strikes accidental? *Economic Journal* 91: 389–404.

Sisson, K. and Taylor, J. (2006) The Advisory, Conciliation and Arbitration Service. In *The Changing Institutional Face of British Employment Relations* (ed. L. Dickens and A. C. Neal). Alphen aan den Rijn: Kluwer Law International.

Smith, A. (1776) *An Inquiry into the Nature and Causes of the Wealth of Nations* (https://www.econlib.org/library/Smith/s mWN.html).

Sorensen, T. (2017) Do firms' wage-setting powers increase during recession? *IZA World of Labor* (https://wol.iza.org/articles/ do-firms-wage-setting-powers-increase-during-recessions).

Sullivan, W. (n.d.) Black workers and trade unions 1945–2000 (http://www.unionhistory.info/britainatwork/narrativedis play.php?type=raceandtradeunions).

Thatcher, M. (1993) *The Downing Street Years* London: Harper Collins.

TUC (2019) Trades Union Councils: who we are and what we do (https://www.tuc.org.uk/sites/default/files/Trades_Councils _Leaflet_2019_A5_AW_No_Details.pdf).

Urwin, P. (2020) Estimating the economic impact of Acas services: April 2018 to March 2019. Update. Acas Research Paper (https://www.acas.org.uk/sites/default/files/2020-09/Estimating-Acas-Economic-Impact-2018-2019-accessible.pdf).

Van der Meer, P. (2019) What makes workers happy: empowerment, unions or both? *European Journal of Industrial Relations* 25(4): 363–76.

Veliziotis, M. (2010) Unionization and sickness absence from work in the UK. ISER Working Paper 2010-15, University of Essex, Institute for Social and Economic Research.

Veliziotis, M. and Vernon, G. (2023) From monopoly to voice effects? British workplace unionism and productivity performance into the new millenium. *British Journal of Industrial Relations* 61(3): 574–94.

Visser, J. (2023) Will they rise again? Four scenarios for the future of trade unions. *Economic and Industrial Democracy* (https://journals.sagepub.com/doi/full/10.1177/0143831X231178850).

Walsworth, S. (2010) Unions and employment growth: the Canadian experience. *Industrial Relations* 49(1): 142–56.

Webb, S. and Webb, B. (1920) *The History of Trade Unionism*, revised edn. London: Longmans, Green and Co (https://www.gutenberg.org/files/66887/66887-h/66887-h.htm).

Whitton, T. (2016) Strife, beer and sandwiches: British trade unions and industrial action during the seventies. In *Le Royaume-Uni à l'épreuve de la crise 1970–1979* (ed. G. Leydier). Paris: Ellipses.

Willman, P., Bryson, A. and Forth, J. (2020) UK unions, collective action and the cost disease. *British Journal of Industrial Relations* 58(2): 447–70.

Wilson, J. H. (1971) *A Personal Record: The Labour Government 1964–1970.* London: Weidenfeld and Nicolson.

Wolmar, C. (2022) *British Rail: A New History.* London: Michael Joseph.

Wooden, M. and Hawke, A. (2000) Unions and employment growth: panel data evidence. *Industrial Relations* 39(1): 88–107.

Wrigley, C. (2007) Industrial relations. In *Work and Pay in 20th Century Britain* (ed. N. Crafts, I. Gazely and A. Newell). Oxford University Press.

Wrigley, C. (2009) Trade unionists and the Labour Party in Britain: the bedrock of success. *Revue Francaise de Civilisation Britannique* XV(2): 59–72.

Wrigley, C. (2015) Labour, labour movements, trade unions and strikes (Great Britain and Ireland). *International Encyclopedia of the First World War* (https://encyclopedia.1914-1918-online .net/article/labour_labour_movements_trade_unions_and _strikes_great_britain_and_ireland).

ABOUT THE IEA

The Institute of Economic Affairs is a research and educational charity (No. CC 235 351). Its mission is to improve understanding of the fundamental institutions of a free society by analysing and expounding the role of markets in solving economic and social problems.

The IEA achieves its mission through:

- a high-quality publishing programme
- conferences, seminars, lectures and other events
- outreach to school and university students
- appearances across print, broadcast and digital media

The IEA, established in 1955 by the late Sir Antony Fisher, is an educational charity, not a political organisation. It is independent of any political party or group and does not carry on activities intended to affect support for any political party or candidate in any election or referendum, or at any other time. It is financed by sales of publications, conference fees and voluntary donations.

In addition to its main series of publications, the IEA publishes the academic journal *Economic Affairs* in partnership with the University of Buckingham.

The IEA is aided in its work by an Academic Advisory Council and a panel of Honorary Fellows. Together with other academics, they review prospective IEA publications, their comments being passed on anonymously to authors. All IEA papers are therefore subject to the same rigorous, independent refereeing process as used by leading academic journals.

IEA publications are often used in classrooms and incorporated into school and university courses. They are also sold throughout the world and often translated and reprinted. The IEA supports and works with a global network of like-minded organisations, through its Initiative for African Trade and Prosperity, EPICENTER and other international programmes.

Views expressed in the IEA's publications are those of the authors, not those of the Institute (which has no corporate view), its Managing Trustees, Academic Advisory Council members or senior staff. Members of the Institute's Academic Advisory Council, Honorary Fellows, Trustees and Staff are listed on the following page.

The Institute gratefully acknowledges financial support for its publications programme and other work from a generous benefaction by the late Professor Ronald Coase.

Other books recently published by the IEA include:

School Choice around the World … And the Lessons We Can Learn
Edited by Pauline Dixon and Steve Humble
ISBN 978-0-255-36779-0; £15.00

School of Thought: 101 Great Liberal Thinkers
Eamonn Butler
ISBN 978-0-255-36776-9; £12.50

Raising the Roof: How to Solve the United Kingdom's Housing Crisis
Edited by Jacob Rees-Mogg and Radomir Tylecote
ISBN 978-0-255-36782-0; £12.50

How Many Light Bulbs Does It Take to Change the World?
Matt Ridley and Stephen Davies
ISBN 978-0-255-36785-1; £10.00

The Henry Fords of Healthcare … Lessons the West Can Learn from the East
Nima Sanandaji
ISBN 978-0-255-36788-2; £10.00

An Introduction to Entrepreneurship
Eamonn Butler
ISBN 978-0-255-36794-3; £12.50

An Introduction to Democracy
Eamonn Butler
ISBN 978-0-255-36797-4; £12.50

Having Your Say: Threats to Free Speech in the 21st Century
Edited by J. R. Shackleton
ISBN 978-0-255-36800-1; £17.50

The Sharing Economy: Its Pitfalls and Promises
Michael C. Munger
ISBN 978-0-255-36791-2; £12.50

An Introduction to Trade and Globalisation
Eamonn Butler
ISBN 978-0-255-36803-2; £12.50

Why Free Speech Matters
Jamie Whyte
ISBN 978-0-255-36806-3; £10.00

The People Paradox: Does the World Have Too Many or Too Few People?
Steven E. Landsburg and Stephen Davies
ISBN 978-0-255-36809-4; £10.00

An Introduction to Economic Inequality
Eamonn Butler
ISBN 978-0-255-36815-5; £10.00

Carbon Conundrum: How to Save Climate Change Policy from Government Failure
Philip Booth and Carlo Stagnaro
ISBN 978-0-255-36812-4; £12.50

Scaling the Heights: Thought Leadership, Liberal Values and the History of The Mont Pelerin Society
Eamonn Butler
ISBN 978-0-255-36818-6; £10.00

Faith in Markets? Abrahamic Religions and Economics
Edited by Benedikt Koehler
ISBN 978-0-255-36824-7; £17.50

Human Nature and World Affairs: An Introduction to Classical Liberalism and International Relations Theory
Edwin van de Haar
ISBN 978-0-255-36827-8; £15.00

The Experience of Free Banking
Edited by Kevin Dowd
ISBN 978-0-255-36830-8; £25.00

Apocalypse Next: The Economics of Global Catastrophic Risks
Stephen Davies
ISBN 978-0-255-36821-6; £17.50

New Paternalism Meets Older Wisdom: Looking to Smith and Hume on Rationality, Welfare and Behavioural Economics
Erik W. Matson
ISBN 978-0-255-36833-9; £12.50

An Introduction to Taxation
Eamonn Butler
ISBN 978-0-255-36836-0; £12.50

Imperial Measurement: A Cost–Benefit Analysis of Western Colonialism
Kristian Niemietz
ISBN 978-0-255-36839-1; £10.00

The Quantity Theory of Money: A New Restatement
Tim Congdon
ISBN 978-0-255-36842-1; £15.00

Other IEA publications

Comprehensive information on other publications and the wider work of the IEA can be found at www.iea.org.uk. To order any publication please see below.

Personal customers

Orders from personal customers should be directed to the IEA:

IEA
2 Lord North Street
Westminster
London SW1P 3LB
Tel: 020 7799 8911
Email: accounts@iea.org.uk

Trade customers

All orders from the book trade should be directed to the IEA's distributor:

Ingram Publisher Services UK
1 Deltic Avenue
Rooksley
Milton Keynes MK13 8LD
Tel: 01752 202301
Email: ipsuk.orders@ingramcontent.com

IEA subscriptions

The IEA offers a subscription service. For £350 a year, UK-based subscribers will receive every book the IEA publishes along with invitations to IEA events – while also supporting the IEA's charitable mission. You can subscribe online by becoming a 'Founding Insider' at insider.iea.org.uk. Otherwise, please contact:

Subscriptions
IEA
2 Lord North Street
Westminster
London SW1P 3LB
Tel: 020 7799 8911
Email: accounts@iea.org.uk